Understanding and Managing Children's Behaviour through Group Work Ages 5–7

Understanding and Managing Children's Behaviour through Group Work Ages 5–7 provides the reader with an insight into children's emotional well-being and helps them to understand what and how children communicate and how to respond in a way that provides positive messages, increases their emotional vocabulary and encourages them to change their behaviour. It provides an alternative and effective child-centred way of managing children's behaviour through introducing the concept of reflective language and other tools, equipping staff with new skills that are transferable across the school in any role.

The book is divided into two sections, enabling the reader to link theory with practice. The first section takes the reader on a journey to help them understand the different factors that influence children's behaviour. The second section of the book focuses on the group work programmes, how they can be used, their value and the impact they can have on children and the school as a whole. The activities in the group work programmes explore the concept of using reflective language as a behaviour management tool and are designed to motivate and build confidence, self-esteem and resilience. Useful pedagogical features throughout the book include:

- practitioner and classroom management tips and reflective tasks;
- strategies and practical ideas for staff to use to help them engage more deeply with the contents of the book;
- flexible, tried and tested group work programmes designed to promote inclusion rather than exclusion;
- clear step-by-step instructions for delivering the group work programmes;
- case studies showing behaviour examples with detailed explanations for the behaviour and strategies to respond to it.

This book is aimed at all Key Stage 1 primary school staff, especially teaching assistants, learning mentors and family workers who can deliver the group work programmes. It is also recommended reading for SENCOs and trainee teachers, and will be useful for therapists who work with children and are looking at delivering other approaches in their work.

Cath Hunter is a therapeutic consultant, trainer and play therapist and has thirty years' experience of working with children, staff and families. Her academic experience includes lecturing on childcare and play work at City College Manchester, and acting as clinical supervisor at Liverpool Hope University. www.therapeuticfamilyinterventions.co.uk

Understanding and Managing Children's Behaviour through Group Work
Ages 5–7
A child-centred programme

Cath Hunter

Routledge
Taylor & Francis Group

LONDON AND NEW YORK

KH

First published 2015
by Routledge
2 Park Square, Milton Park, Abingdon, Oxon OX14 4RN

and by Routledge
711 Third Avenue, New York, NY 10017

Routledge is an imprint of the Taylor & Francis Group, an informa business

British Library Cataloguing in Publication Data
A catalogue record for this book is available from the British Library

Library of Congress Cataloging in Publication Data
Hunter, Cath.
  Understanding and managing children's behaviour through group work
  ages 5–7: a child-centred programme/Cath Hunter.
  pages cm
  1. Classroom management. 2. Problem children – Behavior modification.
  3. Behavior disorders in children. 4. Education, Primary I. Title.
  LB3013.H83 2014
  371.102'4 – dc23

ISBN: 978-1-138-79249-4 (hbk)
ISBN: 978-1-138-79250-0 (pbk)
ISBN: 978-1-315-74064-5 (ebk)

Typeset in Helvetica
by Florence Production Ltd, Stoodleigh, Devon, UK

MIX
Paper from
responsible sources
FSC
www.fsc.org   FSC® C013604

Printed and bound by CPI Group (UK) Ltd, Croydon, CR0 4YY

9/30/15

This book is dedicated to Jessie, Pam and Paula.

Contents

Part One: Theory
A child-centred approach to emotional health and well-being and
understanding children's behaviour

Part Two: Practice
Using group work to promote emotional health and well-being and
manage children's behaviour

List of figures and tables

Figures

Tables

Foreword

There is never an uneventful start of the day in our school and on one of these busy Tuesday mornings, Cath and I stood together watching Jack hurtle down the long and tempting expanse that is our bottom corridor. I shouted 'Jack, walk.' Cath just laughed and said 'Not yet Carol.' And what was Jack's reaction? He was oblivious to us both and carried on as if released from a spinning top. Jack, at that time, had just started in Year 1, he was five years old and had recently started play therapy with Cath.

Sadly, Jack's story, though shocking, is not unusual; born addicted to heroin and never having connected with his birth mother, he lives with his older sister on a residency order. He looked and behaved like a much younger child and spent the school day in solitary but fairly physical activity. Trying to teach Jack was rather like trying to catch water! Enter Cath, her expert advice and calm manner gave Jack space to relax and to discover himself in the safe and undirected environment of the play room. Jack engaged with Cath immediately, though she reported that she needed extra time to tidy the play room after his sessions and every time she walked him back to class he ran ahead of her and we all heard him coming!

Cath stuck with him, she gave advice to his teachers about how to teach him and spent time helping his sister learn about his needs and gently directed her in ways of meeting those needs. When specialists knee-jerked into a diagnosis of ADHD for him, Cath helped me write a letter asking them to wait for the play therapy to work its magic before medicating him.

Jack is one of our individuals with severe difficulties; his life chances were compromised before he was born but with Cath's support we are helping him to catch up. Cath has worked like this in our school and others to help children like Jack and those who are experiencing less severe but still significant challenges in life. She has worked with teachers to develop their skills and knowledge so that they can teach and interact with all children in a calm and effective manner. Her way of working and her sound advice are now accessible to many more teachers and their teams in this easy to follow and ultimately practical guide. Cath writes with authority and, as she does everything, with empathy. Her ideas are easy to implement and tried and tested – they work. She has worked in schools and knows the challenges facing many of us who are trying to provide for children who have become out of kilter with their worlds. She writes so clearly because she has experienced these challenges first hand – her methods are underpinned with specialist knowledge about how children develop and what they need to flourish.

I cannot recommend Cath's book highly enough, its purpose is to help and support those of us who are trying to get it right – it comes from a compassionate place. This book will definitely be joining our staff library.

And what of Jack now? A year on, he walks down the corridor and sits with his peers on the carpet in his classroom. He stays still long enough to listen. He is learning and making progress though he still struggles to grasp ideas that other children of his age manage to understand. Perhaps the biggest indicator of Jack's development is that last week, as Cath and I stood on the corridor talking, he came up to her, hugged her and then in complete charge of himself, walked up to his classroom. Now he has a chance.

Carol Powell
Head teacher

Acknowledgements

I would like to express my thanks and gratitude to the following people who have helped to make this book possible:

The head teachers who employ me and demonstrate their ongoing commitment to understanding, supporting and valuing the work I carry out in their schools.

Carol Powell for her thoughtful contribution in writing the foreword.

The school staff that have the courage and capacity to think about children in a different way and implement the strategies and techniques I suggest during staff consultations and training.

The teaching assistants, learning mentors and family workers in schools who have used this programme, especially Hannah Hayhurst, Sheila Cole and Naisen Berraies for their ongoing dedication to implementing the programmes in school and having a significant impact on the children they have worked with.

Debbie Estkowski, my supervisor, for the many years of support and wisdom she has provided.

Sue Taplin for her time, support and creative contribution to the resources section.

My friends for accepting seeing less of me and supporting me in a variety of different ways.

Jane O'Neill, because I really couldn't have done it without you.

Introduction

For many staff working in primary schools today their desire to support and encourage learning is disrupted by children who do not conform to the expectations of engaged participation in daily school life. We may know of children who refuse to follow instructions, appear to be deliberately disruptive and challenge staff. We may also know of children who are withdrawn, overly eager to please and unable to build and sustain relationships. In some schools there may only be a few children causing concern, in others there may be many. This booked is aimed at helping school staff to understand and support these children and therefore achieve their full potential at school.

For children in our schools who are living with emotional instability and erratic and inconsistent parenting, this is a momentous task. There are also some children who have experienced trauma in their lives to varying degrees, which has a huge impact on their ability to feel safe and results in them experiencing high levels of stress and anxiety on a daily basis. For these children, their ability to settle at school and fully engage with their learning can be severely hampered by the external circumstances they are living in, making the job for school staff an enormous one of meeting emotional needs, managing behaviour and providing a stimulating learning environment.

The purpose of this book is to provide a greater insight into children's behaviour and enable school staff to increase their awareness of what children may be trying to communicate by their behaviour. It is aimed at encouraging different ways of thinking about children and facilitating a better understanding of their difficulties by encouraging school staff to explore the possible meanings behind children's actions. It will focus on increasing understanding of why a child may be doing something, rather than just looking at the behaviour the child is displaying. It also examines the importance of helping children with their feelings instead of just trying to get them to stop their behaviour. The book is divided into two parts to assist the reader to link the theory of supporting emotional health and well-being and improving behaviour with the practical tools to enable school staff to achieve this on a daily basis.

School staff can be confronted with children exhibiting challenging behaviour that ensures they are visible and known to school staff on a regular basis. This book is aimed at exploring the possible reasons why children may be showing these behaviours, along with providing strategies that can be implemented in class to enable them to make positive changes. It is also aimed at raising awareness of children who may be less visible and require additional support to ensure they are noticed and their needs are met. It introduces accessible and successful techniques and strategies for school staff to use to improve children's self-esteem, relational behaviour and promote emotional health and well-being.

I hope it will encourage staff to reflect on a child's behaviour and communications in order to improve understanding and promote a greater awareness of the impact of external circumstances on their mental health and well-being. This knowledge may then affect how adults respond to children, which may in turn positively influence the relationship between staff and children. When adults are open to making small changes in the way they view and respond to children's behaviour, this can have a positive impact on children enabling them to feel more accepted and understood. The techniques and suggestions focus on strengthening the adult–child relationship and may also enable school staff to feel more competent and confident in their role in school.

As children spend a large proportion of their lives at school, they play a crucial role in providing a range of social experiences, as well as having a key part to play in developing resilience in children. Schools play a vital part in both teaching and modelling relationships and life skills to children. When children have difficult experiences outside of school they may not be well equipped to manage school and engage with their learning. The group work programmes focus on equipping children to develop skills such as patience and perseverance, along with the experience of compassion and empathy for others. These essential life skills may not be developed in the child's family, but are essential for them to access the curriculum and achieve at school. Schools are in an ideal position to help them with this and provide them with skills to have a successful life. This book examines the importance of considering children's individual needs and social and emotional needs, which are as important as a child's learning needs and have a huge impact on their ability to engage with their learning.

An awareness and understanding of children's emotional health and well-being is imperative for their general well-being and learning. Children's physical and emotional safety, needs and well-being need to come first and be a priority for schools in order for children to be happy, safe and secure and reach their full potential. In school we may ask children to perform tasks that may expose them or make them feel vulnerable such as reading out loud in class or having a part in an assembly or school play. Children need to feel safe and secure in order to do this. When a child finds it difficult to put their feelings into words they are at a disadvantage at school in terms of making and sustaining friendships and being able to access the curriculum. Children who are able to understand and express their feelings are able to achieve success at school and reach their potential more easily.

Using reflective language is a key concept of this book and in my experience is one of the most powerful tools that can change children's behaviour and set them on the path to improved mental health and well-being. The use of reflective language throughout the book, and particularly in the facilitator's guidelines that accompany each session, can be used with children in any context and provide a different approach to working with children. This unique and easy to use method helps to develop self-awareness, self-control and resilience, all essential ingredients for emotional health and well-being. The staff who have delivered the group work programmes have reported the effectiveness of using this tool both in the sessions and in their other roles around the school as a way of managing behaviour. They have also noticed that their increased self-awareness has resulted in an improved understanding of children's behaviour. The concrete examples of reflective language and staff reflective practice provided enable school staff to become more aware of what, why and how children communicate through their behaviour, along with increasing their awareness of how they respond to this. This change in staff thinking can result in a better understanding of themselves and why they react to certain situations, along with an increased awareness of other school staff. This improved working relationship may result in a positive impact on the children.

I invite all school staff regardless of their role to try the staff strategies and reflections, and explore using reflective language. This may be a new way of behaving for school staff; experiment with it, use it tentatively using words like 'wondering' or 'perhaps' or 'sometimes', rather than 'telling'. While reading this book I encourage you to think about the children you work with on a daily basis and consider what they may be trying to communicate to you by their behaviour. Throughout the book I use 'can' or 'may' to reiterate the importance of remembering that all children are individuals and therefore may respond differently to situations.

I will refer to my own experiences of delivering the group work programmes along with the experiences of staff who have implemented them, as all of the group work activities have been delivered by me and teaching assistants, learning mentors and family workers. The staff delivering the group work felt it enhanced their understanding of children's behaviour and gave them an insight into what the children were trying to communicate. The other school staff including head teachers commented on the noticeable changes in the children after the intervention and felt that it helped them to be more integrated into school life. The group work is most effective when it is delivered as part of a whole school approach to emotional health and well-being.

The group work programmes in this book are tried and tested and have been successfully implemented by school staff in a variety of roles across several schools. They can be delivered easily throughout the school year and provide an ideal opportunity for more focused work for children who need extra support with their social and emotional development. The activities are devised as a six-week programme but can be adapted for use with individuals or pairs of children in a way that meets children's needs. The group work programmes provide an opportunity for children to practise and develop skills, which increase the likelihood of them being socially included rather than excluded from school and society as a whole.

In order to protect the confidentiality of the children and staff, any case studies or examples are composite and names and details have been changed. They are drawn from a number of experiences from my work over several years.

I hope you will enjoy this book and the activities, and that it will enable you to think differently about the children you work with.

Part One: Theory

A child-centred approach to emotional health and well-being and understanding children's behaviour

1 What does a child need to be emotionally healthy?

In order for children to achieve success at school they need a degree of healthy emotional and social development so that they are emotionally ready and able to learn. This involves being able to cope with success and failure and having the resilience to manage this, along with being able to ask for help when they need it. Children aged 5–7 years are often showing signs of becoming more independent and being able to manage separating from their carer, but their ability to do this well is dependent on their early experiences of this. They need to have positive experiences of this separation to be able to manage the school day and all it entails. (I will discuss this further in Chapter Five.) Managing the school day includes having a sense of confidence and self-esteem, having self-reliance appropriate to their age, having a positive self-image and a strong sense of self, along with beginning to be able to understand their own feelings and express them. They need the stability and security to be able to manage change and unpredictability without it eroding their feelings of safety. They also need to have the social skills to develop, build and sustain relationships with both adults and children. How many children are equipped with all the skills to be able to do this?

The experience of being emotionally healthy is achieved by a combination of all these skills together and not in isolation, in the same way as a child's ability to hold a pencil is dependent on their hand–eye co-ordination and manipulative skills. It is the cumulative effect of the child's experiences, learnt behaviours and reactions to events that help define their sense of self and their ability to deal with situations both in and out of school. Children need information and explanations about what is happening in order for them to be able to make sense of their experiences.

Self-regulation

In order for children to be able to regulate their own stress levels, they need to have had this experience from an adult. Babies are unable to regulate their own stress and they depend on their caregivers to regulate it for them. For example, when a baby cries because they are hungry, tired or upset and the adult responds with love and concern, this helps to reduce the baby's stress. If a crying baby is ignored or met with anxiety or hostility, it can increase their stress. The way the adult responds to this stress can either help the child to develop their own stress regulatory system, or create even more stress and prevent this development taking place. If the child gets what they need from an adult then a pattern develops that allows the child to begin to manage stress for themselves.

In order for children to develop healthily, adults need to respond to children's stress in a way that calms and soothes them rather than exacerbates their stress. For example, Tom, aged 3, is happily playing with a train when another child snatches it from him. Tom screams with rage and hits the child. If he is soothed, comforted, listened to and supported then this validates his feelings and enables stress regulatory systems to be developed. If he is offered a calm and clear explanation about not hitting other children then he is gradually able to understand that this behaviour is not acceptable. Tom is totally dependent on the stress regulating systems of a caring adult to help him to develop his own. If a caring adult is able to help him with his feelings and acknowledge and soothe his distress, he gradually develops the ability to do this for himself. As stressful situations occur in his life, he has the ability to manage them due to his initial experiences of stress being held and helped by a caring adult. When a child's parent or carer is able to regulate their own feelings and demonstrate positive and healthy ways of managing their own stress and anxiety, this is beneficial to the child who has this as a template of how to deal with feelings.

However, if the adult responds to the situation by shouting at him, dragging him away or smacking him for hitting the other child, Tom will feel even more stressed and anxious and will be unable to develop self-regulation. He does not learn how to manage stress and anxiety for himself; instead he learns to be wary and fearful of other people and finds it extremely difficult to share. He is overwhelmed by his feelings and unable to self-regulate. He may learn that feelings are to be feared and avoided at all times, rather than managed and expressed in a healthy way.

Case study

Joel, aged 6, had regular tantrums at school where he would scream, shout and lie on the floor crying. He found it very hard if he didn't get his own way and would lash out at other children if they did not do as he wanted.

Possible reasons for Joel's behaviour:

- His parents had a volatile relationship with frequent arguments and physical fights.
- His older brother regularly took his toys and teased him for getting upset and crying.

When children have not had the experience of self-regulation being provided by a parent, school staff can contribute to helping them with this and fulfilling this role.

Strategies to help children to self-regulate

- Respond to the intensity of what the child is feeling and reinforce this with the appropriate tone of voice and facial expression; for example, 'It made you furious that you couldn't be at the front of the line today.'
- Validate the child's experience: it is very real for them so ensure they feel you are taking it seriously; for example, 'When Sam called you stupid it must have really hurt.'
- Support the child by helping them to find alternative ways to express their feelings if appropriate; for example, 'It's never ok to hit people Michael, we need to find other ways that you can have your feelings and not hurt anyone when you have them.'
- Offer a calm and reassuring approach so the child feels you are affirming them and accepting rather than dismissing their feelings; for example, 'It can be really difficult when you want to have the red pen and someone else is already using it.'
- Use regular opportunities during the school day to comment on children's non-verbal signs of emotion; for example, 'I can see you look a bit cross about having to wait your turn.'

The above responses enable the child to feel connected to, understood and recognised for who they are and what they are feeling. It gives the message: 'all feelings are ok and I can help you with them.' It helps them to make the link between feelings and words, which is crucial for children as they can experience their emotions intensely and need help, support and the emotional vocabulary to make sense of what is happening. It affirms the pain the child is feeling and helps them to understand it. This helps them to feel less overwhelmed and alone with the feelings and therefore less scared. This will support the child with developing self-regulation. When an adult intervenes and offers support, it can reduce the anxiety levels for children along with validating rather than invalidating their experiences and feelings.

Children need constant reminders of the behaviour that adults would like to see and explanations of what is expected of them and why. Children require boundaries that can be understood, and therefore it is useful to check their understanding of the rules and expectations that are in place at school and ensure these are clear and realistic to enable all children to experience success. For example, demonstrating how to tidy up rather than assuming all children have the experience of doing this at home. The use of visual reminders can also be a useful way of keeping a connection with a child and enabling them to practise regulating their behaviour.

Staff strategy – visual reminder

Take photos of the child doing the behaviour you would like to see; for example, sitting on the carpet. Show the child the picture of this at the relevant time and frequently throughout the day to help them understand what they need to do.

The role of the facilitator in the group work programmes enables the children in the group to practise self-regulation and provides an opportunity for the facilitator to transfer these new skills to their role across the school. This alternative way of responding to children's feelings and behaviour can be modelled across the school and empowers all staff to use a different approach.

Staff strategy – releasing feelings

If a child needs help to manage their feelings of anger and frustration, offer them a large scribble pad and pens or crayons for them to use when they need to. Ensure they are able to access this easily and offer support and demonstrations if needed.

This activity provides a powerful message that all feelings are acceptable and an alternative and constructive way of helping a child to release them. It can be a useful tool to assist them in the process of self-regulation.

Developing independence

School life and all it entails requires children to have some level of autonomy and to become increasingly independent as they progress through school. An essential developmental task for children aged 5–7 years is the development of independence. The process of separation and independence is a gradual one that school can help with by finding the right balance between nurturing, protecting and guiding children and allowing them to explore and experiment. This enables them to develop some self-sufficiency and security in themselves. The transition to a new class at the start of the school year, coupled with leaving their parent or carer, can be a challenge for even the most secure child. The change from reception class to Key Stage 1 with the focus on more structured learning rather than a play based environment can also be difficult for many children, especially if they have not been encouraged or provided with the opportunity to practise independent skills at home.

A child's ability to develop self-reliance and do things independently depends on several factors and is affected by their confidence and self-esteem along with the opportunity to develop these skills. In school there may be an expectation that children have a level of independence that enables them to cope with the school day. For a child who has no experience of this at home, perhaps because they are treated like a baby to meet their parent's needs, the very experience of this can be daunting.

Case study

Amy, aged 7, was always last to go out at playtime as she could never find her coat. She sometimes found it hard to put it on and could never do the buttons up. She was often found wandering round the cloakroom trying to put on other people's coats.

Possible reasons for Amy's behaviour:

- She was the youngest child of a large family and was seen as the baby and helpless.
- When Amy tried to do things for herself she was discouraged or reprimanded for doing it wrong.

It can be both frustrating and challenging for school staff having a child like Amy in school, but it also provides an ideal opportunity for her to experience support for the essential aspects of her development she has missed out on.

Strategies to promote independence

- Offer opportunities for children to make choices on a regular basis to develop confidence in their own abilities.
- Identify children who need additional help with self-care skills and provide opportunities for this throughout the day.
- Create special jobs for children to build confidence and develop new skills.

When children experience being independent and developing new skills as a positive event that involves them having more freedom, this encourages them to persevere with tasks and situations they may otherwise have found difficult or frustrating. This results in an increased sense of themselves as strong and capable rather than helpless and inadequate. This increases the likelihood of children becoming more independent, resulting in increased confidence, self-esteem and self-belief.

Self-reliance

Case study

Marcus, aged 7, was trying to take his shoe off to get changed for PE. His lace had a big knot in it, which he kept pulling at. The teaching assistant offered to help Marcus but he moved away from her and carried on trying to remove his shoe by himself.

Possible reasons for Marcus's behaviour:

- As a baby if he cried no one came.
- When he fell and hurt himself no one comforted him.
- He frequently looked after his mum who had periods of depression and was often very quiet and absorbed in her own thoughts.

It was impossible for him to ask for or allow himself to receive help as he'd learnt to rely on the only person that had always been there for him, himself. He had learnt to adopt self-reliance as a way of coping and feared neediness or asking for help as it had not been available for him. At school he presented as someone who was self contained and could manage on his own. This resulted in him finding relationships with both children and adults challenging, as he was controlling and manipulative as a way of feeling safe in his world.

In order for children to develop a sense of independence and ability to depend on themselves it helps if they have had an experience of being able to depend on an adult who has responded appropriately to their needs. For a child who has not had this experience or it has been inconsistent, it can feel terrifying to both ask for help and be able to receive it. These children have learnt to be overly reliant on themselves as a way of feeling safe and will need plenty of support to change this behaviour. They may think 'I can only rely on myself.' The challenge for these children is to trust that an adult will consistently support them and to understand that it is acceptable to ask for help from others.

Strategies for children who are overly reliant on themselves:

- Understand that they have learnt to do this as a way of feeling safe and ensure you do not take over or invade their space; for example, provide opportunities for them to work near you so they can access you easily and you can monitor if they need help.
- Identify their need to do things for themselves and reflect on what it may feel like to change this; for example, 'I can see you are struggling to put your gloves on, I wonder what it would feel like if I helped you with it?'
- Let them lead their relationship with you and gradually access help in their own time and at their own pace by gentle reminders that you are available and willing to help them; for example, 'You are working very hard doing that puzzle, remember I can help you at any time if you need it.'
- Provide strong messages that validate it's ok to ask for help; for example, 'Even adults need help with things sometimes and it's ok to ask other people to help us.'

The experience of developing self-reliance and becoming more independent is a gradual process that develops throughout childhood. In order for a child to achieve this in a healthy way it is necessary to provide them with opportunities to experience this.

Strategies to help children develop self-reliance:

- Provide regular opportunities during the day for children to carry out tasks for themselves; for example, getting their own bag and coat at the end of each day.
- Identify opportunities to help other children with small tasks; for example, 'please could you help Chloe tidy the book corner.'
- Ensure that children are rewarded for their efforts as well as their achievements; for example, 'you tried very hard to find your PE kit, well done.'
- Talk to the child's parents and identify something they have done well or achieved that day; encourage them to see the importance of the child having opportunities to do things for themselves at home.

Self-confidence and self-esteem

A child's sense of self-worth is deeply affected by their confidence and self-esteem. For children who have a poor sense of self, the school day can be made up of regular experiences that can erode this even further. It is useful for school staff to consider where a child is in terms of their social and emotional development; for example, are they developmentally 7, or are they still at the toddler age of being unable to share and take turns? If this is the case, they need opportunities to practise and develop these skills during the school day with a sensitive and patient adult. It is important that children's social and emotional developmental levels are assessed to ascertain the additional support they may need, in the same way as their literacy and numeracy levels may be, so the appropriate help can be provided.

Children gain self-esteem from feeling capable and being able to demonstrate new skills, so it is essential to provide regular opportunities for them to experience this. A child with confidence and self-esteem is keen to try new things, may offer to have a lead part in the class assembly and has the ability to develop and maintain good relationships with adults and children alike. They are able to express feelings such as excitement and fear with equal confidence. They have learnt to trust the adults in their lives to care for and support them and therefore have the ability do this for other people. They may believe they are essentially good and likeable and experience other people as the same. There are also frequent opportunities throughout the school day to enhance this and ensure that it is developed to maximise the child's full potential.

However, some children's experiences have resulted in them having a very different sense of themselves. They experience the world as a frightening and unsafe place where it is better not to try new things in case you fail or make a mistake. They have discovered that some adults are unpredictable and that things change frequently and therefore nothing can be relied on. They have learnt that feelings are to be feared and kept to yourself as they can overwhelm you and make things even more frightening. A child with low self-esteem who lacks confidence may present as being unsure of themselves at school. They may resist or find excuses not to try new things and may find it hard to express and manage their feelings. They may believe they are essentially bad and unlikeable and experience other people as better than them and more deserving.

Staff strategy – achievement awards

Do achievement awards to present to children for being kind, thoughtful, etc. Present the award to a child before going home each day, ensuring each child has a chance to receive one at some point during the term.

For example, Kashif has been . . . . today (insert word such as 'helpful').

Strategies to develop confidence and self-esteem:

● Provide opportunities to make choices wherever possible throughout the day, no matter how small; for example, choosing where to sit at times during the day so they feel they have a voice and their opinions are important.

● Identify positive aspects of who they are and how they behave; for example, 'You were really kind when you held the door open for me.'

● Acknowledge and praise them for their achievements and successes no matter how small.

● Introduce emotional vocabulary to them; for example, 'It can make us feel proud when we do something well.'

It is essential to give children the opportunity to make choices, no matter how small, as it gives them positive messages about themselves. It enables them to be assertive and state their wishes in an acceptable way and conveys that they can be trusted to make their own decisions, even if they are different to the ones an adult may choose for them. The experience of feeling that you can be trusted to make your own decisions has a big impact on a child's self-belief and sense of feeling valued and worthwhile, so it is crucial that schools provide as many opportunities for this as possible throughout the school day. It also enables them to have first-hand experience of learning about choices and consequences; for example, if you choose to write with a pen then you can't get rid of what you have written, whereas if you choose to write with a pencil you can.

Children who appear overconfident

There may also be children in school who appear to be overconfident and demand that they are chosen for everything, appear to know all the answers and may present as being happy in themselves. However, this may be a result of needing to be in control and manage situations around them in order to feel safe. This behaviour may be observed in children who have experienced domestic violence or other traumatic experiences and are desperately trying to establish some sense of security and stability in their lives. They may behave in ways that are challenging to school staff such as questioning them and trying to get them to make mistakes or get things wrong. This may be caused by their need to test adults in order to ascertain their reactions to events; for example, 'Miss Brogan always seems very happy, but I am sure I can make her sad if I hit someone.'

This child may have learnt to feel overly responsible for the adults in their lives and need to check out if all adults are unpredictable. While this behaviour can be challenging to deal with at times, it can be useful to explore what may be going on for the child and how they may be feeling. It may be difficult for school staff to accept that children who present as controlling and challenging may actually be feeling frightened and vulnerable. However, if children feel that school staff are unable to manage them they may feel scared and this can reaffirm the negative feelings they already have about themselves.

Strategies for children who appear overconfident

- Remain in charge and be predictable wherever possible, so they feel safe and secure.
- Prepare them in advance for any changes that may occur in order to develop their ability to trust that adults mean what they say.
- Acknowledge and express emotional reactions to things; for example 'Being in a different room can make us feel anxious as we are not used to it.' This may encourage them to begin to voice their own feelings in situations where they feel uncomfortable.

Self-image

Children who have a positive self-image are able to share their happiness about their appearance in a healthy way; for example, showing you their new shoes or haircut. This is an important aspect of children learning to be happy with who they are and along with self-confidence and self-esteem plays a role in self-acceptance. However, for some children this can be a preoccupation and override any sense of the person they are. They may feel that the person they are is defined by how they look and what they wear rather than the qualities and attributes they have. This needs to be handled in a sensitive way by focusing on their personal characteristics.

A child who has a poor self-image may put themselves down by criticising their appearance and making comments such as 'I hate my hair.' This may demonstrate a deeper sense of self-loathing and needs to be monitored closely. They may also have a lack of body awareness and disinterest in their appearance. This may be noticeable if a child has experienced neglect and may be unaware that their clothes or bodies are unclean. These children may be particularly vulnerable to being bullied by other children, especially as they start to become more aware of appearances as they get older. A balance between the two extremes is emotionally healthy, where a child is happy to get themselves and their clothes dirty playing outside but is also happy to wash their hands when they return to class.

Strategies to promote a positive self-image

- Monitor children who avoid messy activities and don't like getting dirty and encourage them to participate by providing aprons and acknowledging their anxieties; for example, 'you seem unsure about getting paint on your hands, remember we can wash them afterwards.'
- Ensure children have a healthy balance between focusing on their appearance and their qualities.
- Share positive comments about children's appearance where relevant and appropriate, without embarrassing them or excluding other children.

Self-belief

Children who have a strong self-belief are able to share their thoughts and ideas and have a sense of determination and perseverance that motivates them to do well. They are able to commit to achieving their goals and work towards them; for example, finishing a piece of work. These children appear to have a drive to do well and are intrinsically motivated to do this. This self-belief is initially developed through external mechanisms such as parental support and encouragement and rewards. This is particularly important for children in early primary who are reliant on the feedback from adults for their sense of self-worth, thrive on praise, acceptance and validation and have often not yet developed an internal sense of self-validation. They also may not have a solid enough sense of who they are to be able to cope with criticism or failure and can find this very difficult to manage without plenty of adult support and reassurance.

Schools can play a crucial role in supporting children who have little or no self-belief, and while this is initially a slow process it is one that is achievable and can make a fundamental difference to children's lives. The development of self-belief initially starts within the family and for a child who lives with criticism, hostility and rejection it is an enormous task to alter what they have learnt and experienced. A child's sense of self-worth can be activated by instilling a sense of them deserving to experience good things in their life; this is difficult but crucial for children who have experienced rejection or who have a sense of themselves as not being good enough. The work of school staff in managing this is immense but achievable.

Strategies to develop self-belief

- Identify attributes you appreciate in children and share these with them; for example, 'I can see you were being really kind when you were helping Matthew find his shoes.'
- Acknowledge children's efforts and attempts at achieving things; for example, 'You tried hard to complete all your writing today, well done for working so well.'
- Introduce motivational vocabulary throughout the day; for example, 'I could see you worked really hard when you were doing the jigsaw today.'

Personal responsibility and self-awareness

An understanding of personal responsibility and self-awareness is necessary for a child to be able to change their behaviour. The combination of both of these enables a child to understand about important concepts such as differences of opinion and acceptance of other people. The ability to accept themselves and their own strengths and areas to work on enables children to develop this same acceptance of other people. This is linked closely with self-regulation, confidence and self-belief, as they are all necessary ingredients for self-awareness and personal responsibility. This concept can be difficult for some children to understand. At approximately 5 years of age children are learning to understand the consequences of their actions, but depending on how this is responded to by the adults in their lives, it can be seen as a positive or negative experience. An activity in the group work programme that focuses on acknowledging differences enables children to see the value in people being different and focuses on the positive side of this. In some families, difference may be seen as something negative and this provides an alternative way to view this.

Staff strategy – two sides to every story

Ask two children to act out a scenario of a playground situation with the children arguing over a ball and ask other children to recap what they saw and heard.

Use this activity to discuss how easy it is to have different versions of the same event and to see things differently. Ask the class to share their experiences of this happening and how it felt.

Self-awareness is crucial to the development of self-control. If a child has an understanding of personal responsibility they are able to acknowledge when they make mistakes and accept accountability for the choices they have made. They have a strong enough sense of themselves to be able to accept that getting things wrong is an important part of learning and to move on from this. They are aware that their behaviour has an impact on other people and are able to recognise when it may be appropriate to change this for other people's benefit. For a child to manage consequences, they need to be able to manage the feelings that may arise from doing something wrong. For example, Josh, aged 6, punches another child who tries to take the ball he is playing with. This results in him being sent in to class and missing the rest of his playtime. In order for Josh to accept the consequences of his behaviour, he needs to be able to experience the feelings of sadness, upset, anger and frustration that may arise from the consequence he has been given. However, he also needs to be able to separate his behaviour from his sense of self; for example, 'I did something wrong but I am still a good person.' For some children, this is where the difficulty lies and why their behaviour may deteriorate into a spiral of negative behaviour after one incident.

For these children, it can be difficult for them to hold on to a positive sense of themselves when they interpret that they are being told the opposite. For example, 'I hurt someone therefore I am a bad person.' They need help and support to tolerate and make sense of the difficult feelings they are experiencing, and this can be helped by an adult acknowledging and exploring some of the possible feelings with them. For example, 'It can make us feel really angry when someone takes something we are playing with, I could see you were playing nicely before that happened. I wonder if it would help if we drew a picture about what happened to help me understand how it made you feel?' This recognition and acceptance of the child's feelings and experience may enable the child to maintain a more positive view of himself both during and after the experience, along with enabling him to accept his consequence more easily.

The concepts of patience, acceptance and honesty can be difficult to understand and implement if this is not your experience outside of school. When children have had no evidence of this experience operating within their family, it may be very difficult for them to grasp. It is important that we spend time explaining these ideas and their meaning to children, rather than assume they already have an understanding. The concept of patience can be linked to mistrust, where having to wait for an outcome may be a frightening experience. The experience of this for some children may be too painful if, for example, your dad suddenly left home one night and you haven't seen or heard from him since and no one has explained to you what is happening or when and if you will see him again. The feelings surrounding this experience may be re-activated whenever the child has to wait for a long time or be patient. If the adults in their family blame each other and other people when things go wrong, or deny anything is their fault as 'things just happen', then it can be very confusing for children to understand the idea of actions having consequences and people having responsibility for the choices they make.

The role of school in providing opportunities for children to understand and gain positive experiences from these ideas is therefore crucial. The whole school ethos can be based around this and linked in to the behaviour and reward system. This is explored in more detail in Chapter Four.

Strategies to develop personal responsibility and self-awareness

- Discuss and celebrate uniqueness and differences between the children and staff in school so children value this as a positive experience.

- Provide opportunities to explore honesty, patience and acceptance so children understand these concepts; for example, 'Let's see how many times we can be patient today class, I want you to help me find examples of when we are doing this.'
- Identify and praise children for their individual choices, especially if they are different to the other children; for example, 'I see you're the only one to have used the green paper Jamie, well done for making the choice that you wanted.'

Resilience

The development of resilience can be viewed as one of the most vital ingredients for emotional health and well-being. The ability to deal with situations and bounce back after adversity is of paramount importance for all children, but especially those who live with uncertainty and disruption outside of school. For children whose lives consist of them being criticised and ridiculed, or who live with drama and chaos, a sense of resilience is necessary for them to cope with this experience. The capacity for anyone to develop and sustain this is supported by the impact of other people who are able to encourage and believe in them.

In order to develop resilience, children need to experience some frustration to enable them to strengthen their ability to problem solve and learn. School staff can support this experience by ensuring they resist the urge to rescue or over help children. While children may not always be able to tolerate frustration, the opportunity to experience this while supported by a trusting adult is vital. The ability to practise having courage and facing fears can also contribute enormously to the development of resilience. A child who has experienced being brave and has had their experience validated by a caring adult is more able to strengthen these skills. Children who are resilient are able to develop strategies to support themselves when they experience difficult situations and therefore have their own bank of resources to use when life becomes challenging. Their experience of using a strategy that has worked for themselves enables them to use this again when they need to.

Strategies to develop resilience

- Provide opportunities for open and honest discussions about how we may feel and how to manage different situations; for example, falling out with friends, doing new things, etc.
- Introduce emotional vocabulary, such as 'scared', 'worried', 'anxious', to enable children to understand and express what they and other people may be feeling.
- Encourage the class to make their own courage creatures out of art materials. Keep these on display and integrate them into lessons and situations; for example, 'Today may be difficult as we've got our tests, you can choose to have them on your desk if you would like to.'
- Acknowledge situations where a child has faced their own challenge and discuss it with them, exploring the skills they feel they used; for example, 'You were very brave when you walked away when Ryan was calling you names and found an adult to tell.'

It is essential that we consider not only how we can develop the resilience necessary for emotional health, but also have awareness of ensuring we do not destroy it. When a child's sense of self is fragile and gradually being developed by positive affirmations of who they are and what they do, we need to be aware of how easy it can be for this to disintegrate by comments, looks, tone of voice, etc. While it is unrealistic and unhealthy to expect children to never be exposed to this, it is useful for school staff to develop a heightened awareness of this and to reflect on how their behaviour may be received by children. This is explored in more detail in Chapters Two and Five.

At school, children are sent out to play at playtime with the assumption that they know what to do and how to do it. Some children have no idea where to start with this and either wander around aimlessly or stand in the corner or attempt to connect with other children and end up in trouble or fights. They do not have the skills or experience to be able to manage relationships with others. Relationship difficulties can flood over from break time to the classroom and interfere with learning. For children to manage school life and all the highs and lows that come with it they need to feel safe in themselves and safe in their world. School provides them with the opportunity to take risks and manage frustration, anxiety and disappointment; all terrifying experiences for children who have no resilience and no positive experiences of this.

Inconsistencies

The experience of erratic and inconsistent parenting where children are provided with extremely rigid rules or no rules at all can make life very frightening and unsafe. For these children, the ability to control what they are able to in school by being manipulative and controlling of other people, including adults, is a strategy they have developed to make themselves feel safe in an ever changing and unpredictable world. For a child who goes home on Monday with paint on his jumper and Mum reacts by laughing, then on Tuesday Mum reacts by screaming, may internalise the message 'no matter what I do I can't get it right.' For these children life can feel full of despair and lacking in hope. This may result in them having extreme reactions to situations; e.g., sobbing and being distraught about a broken pencil. They may have no sense of responsibility and blame other people all the time. Their core belief about themselves may be 'I'm a bad person; I don't deserve to be liked or happy.' They lack confidence, have low self-esteem and poor social skills and may see themselves as worthless and have intense feelings of shame. They may actively set up situations that seek to conform to this distorted sense of themselves. They may refuse to participate as they feel 'what's the point?' and can come across as defiant, aggressive or lazy at school. A stable relationship with a member of school staff may enable them to feel supported and secure.

In families where children are given too much or too little responsibility, they are either never able to be a child or never able to grow up. Children who are given too much responsibility, perhaps by being expected to care for younger siblings, can present as overly responsible and bossy in school. They may also present as always being passive and behaving in a way that demonstrates that their needs aren't important; for example, letting other children go first all the time. The children who are overprotected and never given any responsibility may find it difficult to make choices as they may have little or no sense of who they are and what they like and dislike. Having either an over or under protective parent can be damaging to a child's sense of self and their self-esteem, along with their sense of feeling safe and secure. Children who experience intensely critical parenting by them insisting on perfection, teasing, ridiculing, humiliating the child or shaming or discounting them by name calling or ignoring them, may expect other adults in their lives to respond in the same way. At school these children may be constantly looking for evidence to affirm this negative sense of themselves as worthless.

Differences between home and school

In families where the acceptable way of communicating may be through anger and/or aggression, the social norms and expectations of school are very difficult for children to understand and follow. Children who live in constant fear and turmoil may find it difficult to relax and enjoy school as they are constantly on the lookout for potential danger from other children, adults or the environment, whether these are real or imagined. This constant state of hyper vigilance is very stressful and children in these situations may have learnt that it is not safe to relax as they need to be constantly alert for danger. This has a detrimental effect on their attention and concentration, as well as impairing their social and emotional development.

If children grow up in families where there is often an abundance of drama and lots of stress and excitement around it, they may bring that experience in to school and always be in the middle of every situation, telling long, dramatic and sometimes difficult to follow accounts of other people's behaviour. They may display lots of 'notice me' behaviours such as calling out, sighing, saying they are hurt or unwell and playing the role of victim and 'poor me' extremely well. For these children, it is very difficult to manage the day-to-day life of school without the adrenalin rush of drama and excitement that they are used to, and they may seek to create it for themselves.

The written and unwritten codes of behaviour expected in school can be opposite to the expectations outside of school for some children, resulting in confusion and poor conscience development.

Case study

Kelly, aged 7, would often hit the other children and say hurtful things to them. She would adamantly deny her behaviour even if she was caught by school staff.

Possible reasons for Kelly's behaviour:

- She had learnt at an early age that it was not acceptable to make mistakes and that it was better to lie than tell the truth.
- If she dropped or spilled something at home she was ridiculed and criticised.
- If she hurt her younger brother at home then she was hit and sent to bed.

For children to feel safe, stable and secure, it helps if they have had an experience of this, along with a safe and consistent relationship with an adult. For some children inconsistency and unpredictability are the norm and are familiar to them. They may have experienced parents who although they are physically present are emotionally absent and preoccupied with their own needs and therefore unable or unaware of the needs of their child. These children can find school life extremely challenging where they are unable to hide in the shadows and are brought into the spotlight by their behaviour.

Providing new experiences

In order to change these children's destructive views of themselves, they need plenty of new experiences where the adults are able to affirm their efforts with tasks, even if they don't succeed or complete them, and to be provided with meaningful praise and encouragement. They may be preoccupied with the adult relationships at school and may struggle to focus on tasks and hear instructions. The group work programmes provide the opportunity of being in a small group with a familiar and consistent adult, at the same time and in the same place each week. This experience provides children with an opportunity to experience consistency and predictability. The emotional focus of the group provides children with the opportunity to have their feelings acknowledged and validated rather than ignored or dismissed. If children are not able to express their feelings when they occur, the experience may stay in their body resulting in them feeling stressed, anxious and scared. The opportunity to practise expressing feelings within the group work sessions increases their ability to continue this outside of the sessions.

The group work programmes have been designed to develop children's emotional health and well-being along with providing them with essential skills for everyday life. The facilitator's guidelines to accompany each session focus on identifying, acknowledging and reflecting possible feelings, along with recognising possible difficulties, and praising and encouraging the children for their contributions. This approach enables the children to make links between their feelings and behaviour and experiment with different behaviours in a safe and supportive environment.

Table 1.1 How group work promotes emotional health and well-being

Experience in the group	Potential impact on the child
Children are praised and encouraged	Builds self-esteem
Opportunities to practise and develop new skills	Develops independence and self-reliance
Identifies children's individual qualities	Promotes a positive self-image
Focuses on respecting and exploring differences	Teaches acceptance of self and others
Identifies and acknowledges feelings	Increases emotional vocabulary
Provides permission to get things wrong and make mistakes	Promotes self-acceptance and builds resilience
Celebrates individuality	Develops a sense of self
Identifies and acknowledges effort	Develops a sense of trust
Encourages a commitment to completing tasks	Promotes personal and group responsibility
Encourages children to take risks	Develops self-belief

Children who are emotionally healthy have the skills and ability to tolerate frustration and uncertainty and have a strong sense of themselves as valuable individuals. They are able to relate to others with the skills and confidence to build and develop positive relationships, and have the ability to treat themselves and others with value and respect. They have the skills and resilience to cope with life's disappointments and are able to appreciate and enjoy their own and other people's successes. The group work programmes provide an opportunity for children to practise and develop these skills, which are then transferable outside of the group sessions to the rest of their school life, making the effects of the sessions long lasting.

2 The impact of external circumstances on a child's ability to learn and succeed at school

By the time children start school they have already received strong messages about themselves, other people and the world. They form their initial sense of themselves and how they are perceived as people from within the family, and this can be either positive or negative. A child's internal rulebook is developed early, along with their template of how to build and manage relationships. The family models ways of managing feelings that provides children with experiences that they bring to school and use in their daily life. All of this occurs within the family, which can be seen as the child's first classroom. The more information that school staff are provided with about a child's background and experiences (while maintaining any necessary confidentiality issues), the better equipped they are to respond to the child's needs.

In Chapter One I discussed children needing familiarity, consistency and predictability in order to help them feel safe and secure. How many children experience this outside of school? If children do not feel safe and secure, this impacts on their social and emotional development as well as their ability to settle and engage with their learning at school. They may find it harder to connect and build relationships with other children and adults, and their preoccupation with fear and anxiety can affect their ability to try things and practise and develop new skills.

Physical well-being

There are some children who have many barriers that can prevent them accessing their learning and reaching their potential. If a child's basic needs for food, appropriate clothing and sufficient sleep are not being met they are disadvantaged before they have entered the school building to start their day.

Table 2.1 Potential barriers to learning

Situation	Child is preoccupied with	Impacts on learning
Wearing sandals in winter	Feeling cold	Can't concentrate, shivers, rubs feet
Falling asleep on sofa very late at night	Feeling tired	Yawns, can't engage or retain information, poor concentration, lack of co-ordination, listless, lethargic, fidgety, no resilience, gets upset easily
Missing breakfast and other meals	Feeling hungry, thinking about lunchtime and food	Anxious about the time, fixated with the clock, obsessed with food

Do my needs matter?

All human beings have basic emotional needs for love, validation, acknowledgement and understanding. Within the family a child receives messages about the importance of their needs, and accumulates experiences of how these are responded to. If their needs are responded to consistently by a loving, caring adult who tries to meet them on a regular basis, the child internalises a strong and positive sense of themselves as a worthwhile person whose needs are important and do matter. However, if a child is frequently ignored or met with hostility and resistance when they express their needs, they learn that they are not important or worthwhile and their needs do not matter. A child with this experience may conclude that other people's needs are more important than theirs and will put other people first and try and meet their needs; for example, a child who brings their own ball in to school and gives it to the other children in her class to play with, without playing with it themselves. If children receive the messages 'don't want', 'don't need', 'don't expect', 'don't say much', it is extremely difficult for them to have a positive sense of themselves as a worthwhile person.

Table 2.2 Impact of parent behaviour on child

Parent behaviour	Child learns
Mum is always busy	I must not disturb her
Dad is often out with his friends and doesn't spend time with me	I am not interesting, Dad doesn't like me
Mum frequently shouts and is angry	I must not ask for things or make a fuss
Dad is always bad tempered and unhappy	I must be cheerful and try to make Dad happy
Both parents ignore the child	I am not important or worthwhile
Mum criticises the child on a regular basis	I am a bad person and unlovable

Children who live with these experiences constantly occurring can develop coping strategies as a way of surviving in the world. These may manifest in school by them being controlling, bossy and manipulative, as well as trying to please other people. When a child tries to control the class and challenges adults on a regular basis, they may present as having no fear and not being bothered, but they have developed this behaviour as a way of feeling safe in a world that often feels very unsafe. They may use this coping strategy as a way of managing their feelings; for example, 'If I pretend I don't care then I won't feel hurt or upset.'

Case study

Zane, aged 5, frequently told his teacher that his leg/arm/tummy/head were hurting. He would come in from playtime saying he had banged some part of his body and it was sore. This often disrupted the lessons as he would come over to tell her.

I suggested his teacher offer to spend five minutes with him every lunch time where he could help her prepare the class for the afternoon and I encouraged her to make him a special badge that he wore while he helped her so he would feel important. This enabled Zane to have some individual time and attention where he could talk to her if he wanted to, which provided the message to him that his thoughts and feelings were important. At the end of the first week the number of times Zane was interrupting the lessons and saying he was hurting had drastically reduced and he seemed more settled and happier in himself. The attention he was receiving from his teacher on a daily basis had enabled him to feel noticed and special and he no longer needed to create his own way of getting these needs met.

It's all my fault

Some children may experience themselves as undeserving and may feel overly responsible for things. This may be due to them operating socially and emotionally at a much younger level of development than their chronological age. They may learn that, no matter what they do or how they do it, they are wrong. This can result in them internalising the belief that everything is their fault and they are wrong because they are a bad person. When children hear constant criticism from the adults in their lives they absorb them and believe them to be true, resulting in them developing their own internal critical voice. Consequently, they may have thoughts such as:

- 'I am so bad I make Mum angry all the time.'
- 'I gave my teacher a sore throat because he shouted at me yesterday.'
- 'If I had eaten all my dinner Dad wouldn't have hit Mum.'
- 'If hadn't lost my coat then Mum wouldn't be crying.'

These children live with the contradiction that they can feel both powerful and powerless. They may present in school as being hyper vigilant, noticing everything and being overly concerned with what is happening around them as a way of trying to manage their feelings of anxiety and fear.

Internal belief system

Children develop an internal belief system about themselves by the messages they receive from other people. These messages define whether they are lovable, valuable and worth listening to and spending time with and have a significant influence on a child's confidence, self-esteem, self-belief and how they feel about themselves.

Table 2.3 Developing a positive internal belief system

Parent behaviour	Child feels and internalises the message
Helps child with homework	I am worth helping and I feel good about myself
Attends parents evening	Mum is interested in me and how I am doing at school
Praises child	I am a good person and I can do useful things
Asks child about their day	How I feel is important and I am worth getting to know
Helps child to manage conflict with sibling	Adults can help me

Dealing with contradictions

The family is the place where children learn an initial code of conduct with guidelines, rules and expectations for behaviour. This code of conduct may be in conflict with the behavioural expectations of the school, resulting in the child having to navigate their way through a whole new set of rules. The dilemma for the child may be 'Do I please my parents or my teacher?' Either way this may mean going against or gaining disapproval from one of the significant adults in the child's life. This is particularly difficult for a child who is constantly trying to get it right and please other people as they are stuck in a no-win situation.

The conflict between the different code of conduct between home and school may cause particular problems after school holidays, where the family will have had a much stronger influence over the child due to length of time spent with them. The more differences there are between home and school in terms of expectations and behaviour, the longer and more difficult it may be for the child to adjust to the return to school. If children come from families where things are chaotic and unsettled, rather than calm and peaceful, they may seek to create this at school as it is familiar to them.

Staff strategy – to help children who find school holidays difficult

Provide them with a book and a pen that they can take home and draw pictures or write in it as a way of staying connected to school. They can share the book with you on their return to school if they want to.

This strategy can help a child to hold the memory of school more easily when they are away from it and can help them with the adjustment of returning to school after a break.

Table 2.4 Conflicting messages between home and school

Child's behaviour	Response at home	Response at school
Persistently challenging adults	Adult gives child what they want	Child is reprimanded and kept in at playtime
Has a tantrum	Adult ignores them	Child receives explanation about how to behave
Hits another child	Adult hits them	Child gets age appropriate consequence
Swears	Adult laughs	Child gets name on the board in class
Tries to manipulate and control adult	Adult gives in to child's demands	Child is talked to by teacher who explains about behaviour expectations at school
Interrupting adults	Adult talks louder or shouts	Child is reprimanded and reminded of school rules

If there are no rules or boundaries at home for the child's behaviour, or these are inconsistent and changeable, depending on how the parent feels at the time the child will learn that life can be unpredictable and that adults can be manipulated and controlled at times. For these children, the world can be a very confusing and unsafe place as the code of conduct at home and school are incompatible. If a child has learnt at home that if you challenge adults, plead for your own way and sulk if you don't get it, and adults give in to you, they will try this approach at school, with a very different result for their behaviour.

Child learns

- I can talk back to adults.
- I can do what I want when I want.
- I can manipulate adults to get my own way.
- I can shout when I want something.
- I can interrupt adults to get myself heard.
- I can ignore adults when I choose to.

If a child tries behaviour at school that produces a different outcome at home, it can be very upsetting and confusing for them if it doesn't achieve their desired result. Children who use manipulative, challenging and controlling behaviour at school may have learnt to do this as a way of trying to create their own consistency in an inconsistent world. They are attempting to reproduce an experience that is familiar to them as a way of feeling safe. For example, a child who argues relentlessly that they should be allowed to do PE in their shoes rather than their trainers may have learnt that not only do adults give in eventually, but also 'I am used to being in charge and will do all I can to ensure that it stays that way'.

Children who may have no rules or consequences for their behaviour at home and have lots of freedom may experience school as very restrictive. These children can live in a constant state of high anxiety and it may be difficult for them to manage even very small changes at school. They may constantly oppose authority and struggle to accept inconsistencies happening at school; for example, becoming very upset that you are not doing PE outside: 'But you said we were going outside Miss'. It is crucial that children who experience these difficulties are provided with a sense of predictability and routine and are offered explanations as much as possible in order to reduce their need to try and create this for themselves and allow them to feel safe and settled in school. However, children who come from families who use corporal punishment at home as a way of managing their child's behaviour may feel that the school is too soft and that this has a negative impact on the child's behaviour at school. Equally, the school may feel that the parents approach is too harsh. The result is confusion and anxiety for the child who is caught between the two conflicting approaches.

Case study

Kyle, aged 7, visits his dad in prison every Saturday. He idolises his dad who is in prison for attacking a policeman. Kyle's dad encourages him to 'fight back and not take any messing' from people. Kyle gets distraught and very confused at school when he is in trouble for fighting with other children.

When a child receives attention for negative behaviour, rather than positive, they may view themselves as negative. If a child doesn't get a response from an adult at home when they show or tell them something positive, it can reinforce the message that 'good' behaviour doesn't get a response but 'bad' behaviour does. This can result in the child feeling they need to display negative behaviour to be noticed and get adult attention. If they only receive attention for negative behaviour at home, then at school they receive attention for positive behaviour, they may not understand why the focus is different. A child that is noticed for their 'bad' behaviour rather than their 'good' may conclude that they are bad rather than good. It may reinforce the message that nothing about them is good. The contradictive response they receive at school may confuse them further: 'Am I bad or good? Dad thinks it's funny when I swear, but it makes Mrs Thompson very cross.' It can be an arduous task for schools to undo the early and external messages that children receive about themselves, and while they may be unable to do much to change the child's external world, they are able to change their internal world by providing them with an alternative image of themselves as a good person.

Getting it wrong

The responses that children absorb from home about making mistakes can have a huge influence on their school life on a daily basis. It can impact on a child's ability to try something new, to persevere with something they find difficult and to be honest about getting something wrong. When a child copies another child's work their behaviour may indicate a very fragile sense of themselves, rather than a manipulative controller, which is how they may be perceived. A child who has learnt that it is not safe enough to tell the truth may be so adamant and highly skilled at lying that the member of staff starts to doubt themselves. For this child, the feelings of shame may be overwhelming and need to be avoided at all costs, hence the lying and determination not to be found out.

Case study

Mia, aged 6, appeared to be enjoying being part of the self-esteem group at school. However, for the first three sessions she would offer the pencil to the group facilitator and say 'you do it' when asked to do any of the tasks. Mia was terrified of getting things wrong and had learnt this at an early age when she had been smacked and sent to bed for knocking over a glass of juice.

For Mia, the possibility of getting something wrong was overwhelming and she had learnt that it was better not to try and do things in case she made a mistake or the adults were unhappy with it. She had learnt that it is not ok to make mistakes and when you do, terrifying things happen.
   Mia needs:

- opportunities to make mistakes and get things wrong with an adult on an individual basis who can acknowledge her feelings; e.g., 'It can feel awful when you get something wrong, but everyone makes mistakes sometimes';
- adults to acknowledge their own mistakes to her; e.g., 'I snapped my shoe laces this morning when I was putting my shoes on, but it's ok because accidents happen and I can buy new laces';
- validation of her feelings; e.g., 'It can be really frightening to try and do something if you are worried about what I may say if you get it wrong, but I will be really pleased with you just for trying';
- adults to respond to her attempts to try new things in a positive and reassuring way; e.g., 'You've been very brave trying your new reading book that can feel like a scary thing to do';

- positive responses to her making mistakes; e.g., 'You tried really hard to do those sums even though they were very difficult for you, it's ok to get things wrong, well done for trying'.

When a child behaves in this way it can have a big impact on their learning and ability to make and sustain friendships with other children. If a child is scared of trying things for fear of getting it wrong they may find it difficult to start things, be disruptive, disengaged and tell lies. They may also sabotage the situation; for example, being rude and aggressive to the teacher the morning of a school trip so they are not allowed to go. The child may have learnt that feelings of disappointment are easier to manage than the fear of new experiences. Children who sabotage things may believe 'Good things can't happen to me, I don't deserve to have nice things happening.'

Learning how to manage feelings

The reactions to feelings and how they are acknowledged and expressed within the family provides children with a template that they may replicate at school. As discussed in Chapter One, self-regulation and the ability to identify and respond to feelings is learnt in childhood and carried on into adulthood. Children learn self-regulation by having an adult who can help them to identify, name and express their feelings. Children learn this at a very young age as babies' brains are still developing and are very sensitive to stress and are unable to regulate their own stress and depend on their carers to regulate it for them. The way that adults respond to this stress can either soothe and alleviate it or exacerbate it. If they are responded to in a way that soothes it, they gradually develop their own stress management system. If they receive what they need they become able to manage the stress more easily themselves. However, if the adult responds in a way that increases the stress, it can heighten the anxiety levels and prevent this development taking place. If children do not receive soothing from an adult in times of distress and upset they do not develop their own stress regulating system, unless another significant adult takes on these vital parental functions with the child on a regular basis. School staff can play a vital role in helping children learn to understand and express their feelings and therefore develop self-regulation.

If a child has not learnt self-regulation, it can have an enormous impact on their learning and relationships at school. They may become involved in arguments and fights with other children and may be unable to accept or deal with the feelings evoked by this. This can also affect their ability to be able to focus and engage with their learning as they may be preoccupied with trying to manage their feelings. Their inability to self-regulate may affect their friendships with other children and relationships with school staff. It may also be more difficult for them to be involved in extracurricular activities such as sports clubs due to their difficulties in managing competition and failure.

The way that the adults in the child's family respond to and demonstrate managing their own feelings impact on how children learn to do this and the messages they receive about how acceptable this is. This may also be in conflict with school and the messages they receive there. For example, how do the child's parents express anger and frustration?

All the situations in Table 2.5 (page 24) are terrifying for children who may learn that feelings are not good things to have and should be avoided. When children express their feelings in ways that contradict the norms of behaviour at home, this may result in them experiencing being humiliated, shamed and ridiculed. For example, a 7-year-old boy who cries may experience teasing from family members and internalise strong messages about this such as 'I need to be strong and not show my feelings, crying is a sign of weakness and failure.' When children learn to hold on to their feelings and not express them it can be very difficult for them to change this behaviour. They may develop a 'don't care' attitude to learning, friendships and school, which can be a learnt response to avoiding having to deal with feelings. Children who have learnt to suppress their feelings may believe that they should not have them and certainly should not show them.

Table 2.5 Expressing feelings in the family

Situation	Feeling	Expressed by parent
Post office is closed	Anger	Punches the wall outside the shop
Can't open a jar	Frustration	Throws it across the room
Has an argument with a friend	Sadness	Gets drunk
Will be late for an appointment	Anxiety	Shouts and screams at the bus driver

Within the family children witness reactions to everyday events, and these may affect their responses to drama and excitement. If a child experiences excitement, drama and attention from everyday events involving relationships and conflict, they learn that drama is important and this is how to get a response from the adults around them. They may start to recreate this in school as it is familiar and they may crave the adrenalin and excitement that dramatic events can provide. For example, a child may return to class after playtime with a long and complicated story that involves lots of people and events. The teacher may not react in the way the child is expecting who therefore doesn't get the response they were looking for. The child may then proceed to create more drama by being disruptive and interrupting the lesson to get the attention they are craving. They may become overly involved in what other people are doing and provide commentaries on it. They may find it hard to just stick to the facts in events and not add their own fabrication, which they think may result in them getting more attention.

Case study

Tara, aged 7, came from a large and prominent family in her local community. Both her parents had regular conflict with the neighbours, local families and other parents at the school. They were both frequent visitors to the school where they would challenge staff and demand an immediate meeting with the head teacher. After most lunchtimes Tara would have a story she urgently had to share with her teacher. They always involved several people, including lunchtime organisers and a series of events that were sometimes hard to follow. The class teacher was often amazed at how much could happen in a single lunchtime.

Tara needs:

● opportunities to develop confidence and feel good about herself without the need to create drama;
● a special job that can make her feel valued and enable her to contribute to the class, such as looking after the book corner;
● an adult to spend time helping her understand alternative ways of managing conflicts and building relationships.

Parental expectations

Parents will bring their own experiences of schooling and their attitude towards education and learning with them in to school. It is essential that school staff are aware of this and the potential impact it can have on the parent's ability to fully engage with and support their child's learning. If a child's parents have negative experiences of school and staff from their own childhood then it can take a great deal of courage to even walk through the school gates, let alone speak to teachers or approach the head teacher. If a child's parents are consistently avoiding entering the school it can be useful to explore the possible reasons for this and offer alternative times to talk to them if possible. There may be numerous reasons for this; for example, they may feel overwhelmed by the other parents, particularly if they experience them as loud and domineering.

Reflect: How do you experience parents?

Think about how you experience parents who are challenging or may be experiencing difficulties with school and ask yourself if you would be happy to wait around in the playground to talk to them?

Some parents may believe that school is a waste of time and that children don't learn anything. They may think that school staff are too strict or too soft and say things like 'it never did me any good.' They may keep their children off school, not wake them up in the morning so the children are late, discourage them from doing their reading, refuse to pay for school trips and never send the child's PE kit in. These parents are more difficult to engage with the school and their child's learning and may require additional support from a family worker or attendance officer if they are available through the school.

Case study

Emma was the parent of three children and had found her own school days to be very difficult as she was extremely shy and had been bullied by a large group of girls for many years. She had experienced the school staff as only being interested in the bright and lively pupils and after eventually finding the courage to tell one of them about being bullied, was dismissed as wasting the teacher's time. Emma then played truant regularly and stopped going altogether on her sixteenth birthday. She had left school with no qualifications and wanted her own children to do well at school. She was mistrustful of all school staff and appeared aggressive and volatile at times. She would rush in, shout at the children to hurry up and then chase them out of the school building. The school staff thought she was rude and disinterested in her children's education, and were amazed that the children all produced their homework on time and had their reading records signed every night.

The parent's relationship with their child

A useful indicator of both a parent's relationship with school and their child is how they meet and greet each other at the start and end of the school day. Does the child bring themselves and their siblings in to school alone, sometimes arriving too late or too early? Or are they brought to school by Mum or Dad who kisses them and tells them to have a good day? This start of the school day can impact enormously on the child's ability to settle in to class easily and engage with their learning. How are they greeted if they are collected by the parent at the end of the day – are they acknowledged or met with scowls and reprimands such as 'what's that on your jumper?' If the child shows the parent a certificate or picture they have made, does the parent respond or just carry on talking to another parent or continue their conversation on their mobile phone? All these responses provide children with messages about how loved, valued and important they are.

If a parent is critical and judgemental towards their child, the child learns 'I am not good enough, I can't get it right, it's not ok to be me, and there must be something wrong with me.' These can all have a strong impact on their self-esteem and self-worth and over time may gradually erode their sense of self. If a child feels unloved and unlovable as a result of the messages they receive they may seek external gratification through food, bullying others, and being demanding and clingy to school staff as a way to manage their feelings. This can all have a significant impact on the child's behaviour.

Table 2.6 Development of internal belief system

Child feels	Child learns	Child behaves
I'm not good enough	I am worthless	Tries to make other people happy
I can't get it right	I need to try harder	Tries to be perfect
It's not ok to make mistakes	I need to be perfect	Is bossy, manipulative, controlling
It's not ok to be me	I need to be different/someone else	Is always putting other people's needs before their own

Additional pressures on parents

The external difficulties that some parents may be dealing with on a daily basis may result in them not being able to meet the emotional needs of their children, however much they may want to. The impact of situations such as domestic violence, poverty, bereavement, poor housing and drug and alcohol dependency may all result in a parent being stressed, anxious and preoccupied with their own problems. This may mean they are physically and/or emotionally unavailable for the child and may find it difficult to engage with the child's emotional needs. When a parent is stressed they may have no capacity to understand or meet the child's feelings as they can be too overwhelmed by their own. The parent may want to be able to do this for their child, but their own practical and emotional difficulties may be barriers to them being able to do this. Unfortunately, when children are living in circumstances like this, they can respond to the anxiety and stress by becoming more insecure and anxious themselves, creating another stress for the parent to manage.

Case study

Margaret had five children and was frequently complaining about the school and the way her children were treated. The school staff found her challenging and would turn around and start walking the other way if they saw her on the corridor, rather than face the torrent of negativity she sometimes had waiting for them. Since her youngest child had started full time at the school nursery, Margaret had found her days long and empty. She was at her happiest during the school holidays or if one of the children was unwell and had to stay at home with her.

The head teacher approached Margaret and asked her if she would be willing to help organise and repair books in the school library with another parent as the school staff were struggling to find the time to do this. Margaret resisted at first but eventually agreed to 'give it a go'. The role created for her by the head teacher made her feel important, valued and that she had a purpose. She became more positive towards the school, seemed happier in herself and eventually started working as a lunchtime organiser.

The opportunity provided by this school enabled Margaret to realise she had something to offer and was able to contribute and receive attention in a positive way. It also enabled her to use her skills as a parent to find work.

The impact of domestic violence on children

When a child is living in a stressful situation such as domestic violence, their home can become a terrifying and unpredictable place, rather than a haven of security. The significant impact on children of living in these circumstances and the enormity of the problem can be hard to comprehend. A child may be preoccupied with what is happening at home and unable to engage with their learning. They may have difficulty retaining information and appear to be in their own world a lot of the time. If children live with fear it may affect their ability to hear instructions; for example, a child going to their drawer and just standing and staring into space as they are unable to remember what they needed to do. Some children may pretend they are unwell and need to be sent home as a way of trying to check what is going on or staying at home to stop it happening. A child may deliberately forget his PE kit so the school will phone Mum to bring it in as a way of checking that she is safe.

Some children may have negative associations of mealtimes as this may be when the violence occurs, and they may either eat very fast to get away from the situation or pretend they are not hungry. They may have learnt to accept feeling hungry as mealtimes at home are often disrupted due to fights and violence. A child who has experienced domestic violence may also come across as being very vigilant as they may have learnt to be watchful as a way of trying to stay safe. Living with domestic violence may result in some children finding it difficult to make friends and manage relationships, due to confusion over what is acceptable and unacceptable behaviour. They may become quiet and withdrawn or become loud and fidgety with poor concentration. They may feel angry, confused, anxious, insecure and frightened. This may result in them having nightmares, being more tired than usual due to disturbed or lack of sleep.

Children who grow up in a family where there is domestic violence may learn powerful lessons about the use of control, intimidation and force in relationships. They can learn that aggression is part of everyday life and it is acceptable to shout at and hit other people. This can make it very confusing and difficult when they are at school where this behaviour is not seen as acceptable. They may try to placate school staff as they have learnt to try and please other people as a way of trying to control the situation. Children who live with domestic violence may not experience positive relationships being modelled as they may have one parent who is the controlling aggressor and the other parent who is the terrified victim. This may make it hard for either parent to be consistently physically or emotionally available for the child, resulting in the family being a very frightening place at times.

Responsibility

Some children may have responsibilities for younger siblings, themselves and their parents, as a result of the adults in the family being unable to fulfil this caring role.

A child may take on a caring role for younger siblings, which can involve getting them ready for school, making breakfast, bringing them to and from school and taking on the parenting role within the family; for example, a 7-year-old who goes on his bike to the corner shop at 7.30 am to buy bread so all the children can have toast before they go to school. Children may be involved in the financial concerns of the family and be aware of money worries, which in turn become their worries. For example, a 7-year-old boy who told me 'We've not got any money till Thursday so we're just having toast for our tea.' This knowledge of his family's money concerns created huge anxiety for this child and he was often preoccupied (possibly with hunger) and anxious to please other people and therefore unable to fully engage with his learning.

Multiple transitions

For most children, managing daily school life with its challenges and changes along with moving to a new class at the end of each school year is enough to deal with. There are some children who along with this also move schools frequently for a multitude of reasons, including parents moving house, either through choice or necessity due to being re-housed. For these children, the difficulties of dealing with school life on a daily basis are compounded. They may have had to move away from other family members and the community they are familiar with and start again on a regular basis. I have worked with a child who had moved from one school to another and back to the original school and then moved again, all within the space of less than two years. For this child, her ability to settle at school, manage the daily routine and build and maintain friendships became impossible. She was living with high levels of anxiety and was scared and confused, especially as her actual leaving day kept being changed.

Staff strategy – transition activity to help a child adjust to their new school

Story – Ask the child to create a story using words and pictures; e.g., This is Fred (draw a stick man), this is his new school (draw a building). I wonder how Fred might be feeling (angry/scared/excited). I wonder what he might do. This is Fred's new teacher, etc.

When children live with this uncertainty and lack of consistency and security, it can be difficult for school to be the secure base it needs to be. The varied approaches that the different schools may have can result in the child feeling overwhelmed, unable to access learning and falling further behind with each change of school. This can impact on their confidence and self-esteem along with their ability to build and sustain friendships. This may result in them being more vulnerable to being bullied or becoming bullies themselves as a way of feeling more powerful in response to a situation that often renders them powerless. They may position themselves on the margins of school life as they are unsure how long they will be staying at a school and therefore can resist efforts made by school staff to help them settle. This is discussed in more detail in Chapter Five.

Staff strategy – helping a child settle

Identify a key person to be allocated to any new child to help them settle in to the class and the school. Make a welcome book for them with photos of them around the school with situations chosen by them. Allow them as much choice as possible and allow them to build relationships with adults and staff gradually, in their own time and at their own pace.

The wider community

Just as there can be differences between the code of conduct between home and school, this can be reinforced by the wider community that children are living in. There can be hierarchies of power between families and this experience may result in people living in fear; for example, an adult being scared to report the domestic violence they hear from their neighbours every night for fear of reprisals. There may be a different moral code that children are dealing with that may conflict with school; for example, a child who is asked not to lie, cheat or steal at school, but knows that their mum puts nappies under the bottom of the pushchair and walks out of the shop without paying for them. This child can be in conflict about what is right and wrong and may be unclear about how to get it right themselves: is it ok to steal food if you are hungry or take nappies if you haven't got any money?

Schools face an enormous task of trying to change some of the behaviours that are aspired to and validated by the wider community in some areas. The way in which status and power is achieved and recognised in some communities may be very different to the experience that schools are trying to encourage children to develop. Is it good to be clever or do you have to be naughty to be noticed? It is a complex task to try and understand the impact this can have on children in terms of who they are and the expectations and code of conduct from the community versus school. There are different gender pressures on girls and boys and these can be in conflict with who the child is and the strengths and abilities the school is actively encouraging the child to pursue. For example, a boy who excels at singing or dance may not be encouraged by his family or the community to pursue this talent. The child can be caught in conflict of trying to gain approval from three external areas.

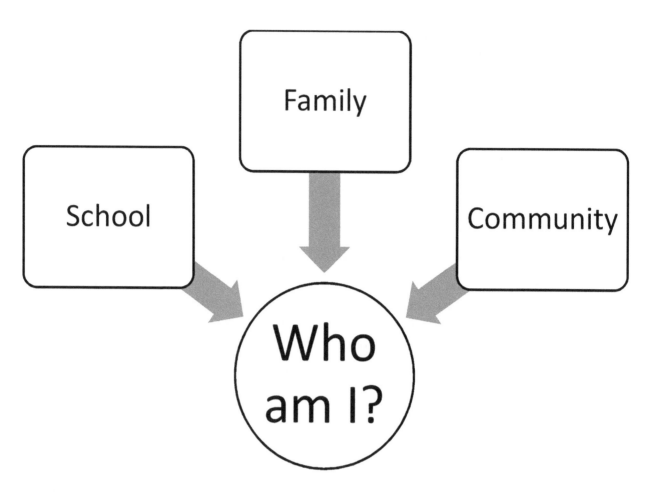

Figure 2.1 Who am I?

Some schools are operating in communities where there may be three or more generations of the same family living there who have never worked. The children in the family may never have known a family member who has worked. This can be in direct contrast to the messages of the school about working hard: how do we encourage children to integrate this message without saying that school is right and their family is wrong?

It can be very hard to develop aspirations, determination and motivation to succeed, along with a sense of purpose and having goals for children who may have only experienced the opposite outside of school. It can be difficult to inspire children to be the best of who they are and reach their full potential when it may conflict so strongly with the messages of their family and wider community. It is our responsibility to help generations of families to break this cycle.

3 What is this child trying to tell me?

Every child wants to be seen, known, valued and understood, but sadly for some children their behaviour can result in them getting the opposite of what they need. If a child is being disruptive, picking fights, being uncooperative and challenging school staff, or if a child is constantly trying to please other people, they are very clearly trying to communicate something to the adults around them. Most adults use language to express their needs and how they feel to other people. Most children, however, do not have the same language skills as adults and use behaviour to communicate their feelings. They need help from sensitive adults to help them work out and express what they feel. Every behaviour is trying to tell us something; for example, a tantrum may be communicating fear, frustration, boredom or anger. A child who is disruptive and challenging to school staff may be ensuring that he gets noticed and is not forgotten about or overlooked. It is the adult's role to try and understand what the child may be trying to tell them and then to respond accordingly.

How adults and children communicate

Reflect: Compare the two scenarios

Scenario 1

You are a class teacher for Year 1 and you had an argument with your partner before you left for work this morning, resulting in you arriving at school late and unprepared.

- How easy would you find it to settle at work and perform well?
- What would you be thinking and feeling?
- What could you do about this?
- How could you communicate your feelings and get support?

Scenario 2

You are 7 years old and you had an argument with your mum before you left for school this morning, resulting in you arriving late to school without your homework.

- How easy would you find it to settle in to class and engage with your learning?
- What would you be thinking and feeling?
- What could you do about this?
- How could you communicate your feelings and get support?

Sometimes as adults we can forget that we have the benefit of experience, developed language skills and the ability to articulate our thoughts and feelings if we choose to. We are able to rationalise experiences and know that we will survive them. We have strategies to solve difficult situations and the benefit of life experiences to know that things usually pass and life does not stay challenging forever. We can choose to talk to people and get support if and when we need it. How difficult are any of these for a 7-year-old to do? Is it therefore surprising that they communicate their feelings and need for support through their behaviour? As adults, the more understanding we can have of what a child may be trying to communicate to us through their behaviour, the greater the chance of the child being understood and being able to make sense of their thoughts and feelings and the more compassion adults can have for them. Children are often very alone with overwhelming thoughts and feelings, and this can be a lonely and terrifying experience.

Children communicate a range of different feelings through their behaviour and these can be expressed in many different ways; for example, if a child is scared they may hide under the table or pretend they are not bothered.

Table 3.1 Understanding behaviour

Behaviour	Possible feeling
Hiding under table	Scared
Following adult around school	Lonely
Throwing objects	Angry
Hitting someone	Frustrated
Fiddling with something	Anxious
Challenging an adult	Terrified
Criticising another child	Jealous
Saying they don't care	Embarrassed
Chewing their jumper	Worried
Copying another child's work	Sense of failure

Children's internal dialogue

Some children may have learnt to respond in a defensive way as a coping mechanism to manage the feelings of anxiety and fear that situations evoke in them. The child may present as feeling the opposite of this; for example, not scared and not bothered, but he may have learnt to do this as a way of not feeling pain. 'If I pretend I don't care then I can't be hurt or feel pain.' For this child the silent pain of feeling unwanted or unloved can result in them feeling isolated, confused, frightened and alone. They may feel that everything that happens is their fault and have an internal dialogue that asks 'Am I a bad person? Am I unlovable? Why do I get it wrong all the time? Why can't I do anything right?' When children have this internal belief system and are convinced that they do not deserve anything good, they may go to extreme lengths to prove it.

The combination of their feelings of low self-worth along with a negative internal dialogue not surprisingly may result in challenging and disruptive behaviour as the child tries to bury their feelings and silence their internal voice. They may also actively try to sabotage situations to recreate the feelings and experiences that are familiar to them. Children who have a negative internal dialogue may believe that adults do not like them when they reprimand them. These children may find it difficult to hold on to positive thoughts about themselves as they do not have an internal view of themselves as a good person. School staff can play an essential role in helping to rewrite their internal scripts into a positive dialogue. For example, 'If Mrs. Hawkins thinks I'm a kind person maybe I am.' It is crucial that we focus on the positives for these children, no matter how hard this may be to implement and sustain.

Case study

Nathan, aged 5, was often late for school and would swear at school staff and run off when challenged about his behaviour. He found it difficult to manage any relationships with the other children as he was unpredictable and would lash out and hit them, often laughing as he did this. The school staff were finding his behaviour very difficult to manage and were also concerned about his physical safety as he would sometimes hide around the school.

Possible reasons for Nathan's behaviour:

- His dad had died recently and his mum was finding it hard to cope with him and his younger sister.
- Nathan was terrified that his mum might die too and he did not know how to express his feelings.
- He was worried about his mum when he was at school because she kept crying all the time and was very sad.

When children show us behaviour that can be challenging and difficult to manage it can be hard to consider that behind the behaviour may be feelings of fear and terror. Children like Nathan may be easily misunderstood in our schools and it can be a complex task to try and understand the possible feelings behind the behaviour. It can be difficult to imagine a child may be feeling fragile and vulnerable when their behaviour appears to be showing us the opposite of this. It can be a challenge for adults to look beyond the child's behaviour and see the pain underneath. If a child is demonstrating difficult and unmanageable behaviour, they may be showing us that they are having difficult and unmanageable feelings and that they need help with them.

Responding to behaviour

Children do not want negative comments or attention for challenging behaviour, but some children may have learnt that any attention is better than no attention and therefore may evoke negative reactions from adults. Children who seek attention in the form of disapproval because they believe they will not gain attention in the form of approval may be showing us they have low self-esteem and may believe that other people are unable to see the good in them. For example, a child that constantly calls out in class may be doing this behaviour to ensure that they stay noticed. It is a guaranteed way of ensuring that they receive attention and are remembered. This may tell us about the child's experiences outside of school: why do they need to ensure that they are noticed and remembered at school? Do they have a different experience at home? When children are happy and settled they do not need to ensure that adults notice and remember them; if they do this it is an indication that they need additional help and support.

It can be hard for some children to tolerate their feelings and this can result in them trying to get rid of them rather than accepting and trying to understand and process them. For example, a child who is unable to manage feeling angry may hit another child or throw something as a way of trying to get rid of that feeling. When a child picks on or bullies another child it may make them feel big and powerful and can be an opportunity for them to feel strong, albeit for a short amount of time. Children need help and support from adults to realise that it is natural to have feelings and that they can be helped to understand how to recognise and express them. It can be useful to integrate positive messages about feelings throughout the school day such as 'All feelings are useful as they tell us something is wrong.' This validates their experiences and normalises how children may be feeling. Some children have little resilience to cope with their feelings, and events that can happen during the course of a school day can feel too difficult for them to manage, such as losing a game or not being at the front of the line. I recently heard of a 7-year-old who burst into tears in assembly when another child from her class was presented with an award. Experiences such as these can be interpreted by children to mean that they are special, important and good enough. For children who have a fragile sense of themselves it can feel overwhelming to imagine someone else being chosen instead.

This following activity can be integrated in to the school day and carried out with the whole class to help them settle after break or lunchtime or when they are anxious or unsettled. It can take about five minutes but can be longer or shorter to suit the time available. If children laugh or mess about they may be showing that they feel uncomfortable and it can help to acknowledge this by saying 'This may feel a bit strange at first but let's practise it as I think it will help us feel more relaxed.' If this behaviour continues they are showing you they need more help with this so could practise it in a smaller group with an adult.

Staff strategy – a grounding activity to help children feel settled

Ask each child to find a space by their table or on the carpet and stand with their feet slightly apart. They can choose whether to have their eyes open or closed. Ask them to focus on their feet, noticing how each toe feels and guide them through this: how does your left foot feel, focus on your little toe, then the toe next to it, etc. Now focus on your left knee, notice how it feels, then your right knee, now your stomach, left arm, right arm, left hand, each finger, left shoulder, right shoulder, neck, left ear, right ear. Ask the children to notice how it feels after you have named each body part.

Use a quiet and gentle voice throughout the activity

End the activity asking them to do a very gentle stretch with both arms and smile.

For school staff it can be a huge challenge to look beyond the behaviour and attempt to understand what the child may be feeling. It can be easy to judge children for their behaviour as the following comments demonstrate:

- He's just attention seeking.
- She's being manipulative.
- He never stops talking.
- She's such a good child.
- He's so helpful.
- She's so immature.
- He never speaks.
- She never listens.

However, if adults are able to meet a child's need to be noticed and remembered in a positive and supportive way they may reduce or even stop the behaviour. For example, 'I know it's really hard for you to listen carefully so I am going to give you something to remind you and help you to practise this.'

Staff strategy – helping a child to listen carefully

If a child finds it hard to listen, put a picture of an ear laminated on the child's table to remind them to use their ears. Acknowledge and reward them for their efforts and achievements with this.

This activity gives the child something to focus on and can help to reduce their anxiety. It may also meet their need to be noticed as they have a connection to the adult through the picture along with the acknowledgement of their efforts and achievements. After a while the child may learn and start to trust that they are able to get help from an adult with their feelings and to be remembered without having to remind staff.

What are children trying to communicate?

When children show us their feelings through their behaviour it is important that we not only try to understand what they may be feeling and trying to communicate to us, but also that we provide them with an emotional vocabulary to help them to talk about their experiences. For example, when a child says they do not want to do something they may be telling us they are scared. How often as adults may we decide we don't want to do something when the real reason may be that we are scared? It can be useful to respond by saying, 'I know you are saying that you don't want to do that, but sometimes it can feel a bit frightening to try new things.' Although the child may adamantly deny they are experiencing any fear, it is still helpful to tentatively introduce the idea that this can sometimes contribute to our resistance. If a child uses a baby voice to ask for something or talk to us they may be telling us they are feeling small and vulnerable. It can be helpful to consider what the emotional age of the child is and whether it would be useful to respond as you would with a younger child. When a child fidgets, rocks on their chair, taps things or wriggles on the carpet they are again telling us something. It may be they are telling us they feel worried, anxious or stressed. A response such as 'I can see you are finding it hard to stay still at the moment' can be enough to help a child relax as it communicates that you have noticed them without reprimanding them. It is also important to consider the child's non-verbal communication such as their breathing: is it shallow or does it quicken when they are asked to do certain tasks? A teacher told me recently of a 7-year-old who sighs heavily when she asks him to get his reading book. He is clearly communicating his anxiety about this task.

Staff strategy – find the feeling

To help children to identify how they feel, use a feelings board at regular intervals during the day. Ask them to draw a face under the word in each box to show the feeling and attach an arrow with a paper fastener in the middle of the square. Ask the child to move the arrow to the relevant feeling.

Happy	Sad

Angry	Scared

This can help children to connect with their feelings more easily and provide permission for the child to experience all their feelings as acceptable. It can provide a useful stepping stone for children who need more support in linking facial expressions with actual feelings.

Helping children to reconnect

Children who live in noisy and chaotic families may tune out and be in their own world as a way of finding some internal peace. At school they may appear not to be listening and may seem disengaged and disinterested. If a child has developed this behaviour as a coping strategy in order to make it easier to live with chaos, we need to be supportive to this and ensure we approach it sensitively. For example, gentle reminders such as a tap on the arm can help them to reconnect with the present moment. The school staff's increased awareness of the possible reasons behind children's behaviour can ensure they offer the appropriate support for the situation. For example, if a child says they feel unwell on a regular basis it may be an indication of stress or anxiety. Children may find it hard to differentiate between physical and emotional pain, they just know they do not feel well. Expressions such as 'sick with fear' are realistic for children who do not have the emotional vocabulary or understanding to separate physical from emotional discomfort.

Table 3.2 Links between physical and emotional well-being

Physical feeling	Possible emotional reason
Headache	Worried
Sickness	Fear
Stomach ache	Anxiety

Children may create their own rituals which they demonstrate at school to enable them to feel secure, such as going to the toilet at a particular time of the day or having to sit on the same chair. This behaviour may indicate anxiety and fear and will only be alleviated when the child feels safer. Wherever possible, unless it impacts on another child, it will help the child if this behaviour can be accepted and attention given to helping them feel settled and secure, rather than trying to change their behaviour.

Children who hurt themselves and cry for a long time and find it hard to be comforted, or children who do not seek comfort or show any distress when they have been hurt, can both be indicative of a need for further support. If a child has learnt to self-soothe it may be that the adults have not been physically or emotionally available to help them with their feelings. It can be helpful to acknowledge this by saying 'In school there are lots of adults who care for you, you can always tell us if you are hurt and we will try and make it better.' This provides a strong message to the child that the adults will help them and look after them.

Staff strategy – feeling settled

Offer an object such as a small figure or animal to the child to look after during the day and keep in their drawer overnight. This can help a child to feel more settled and safer at school. Encourage them to give it a name if they wish to provide them with a sense of ownership.

The object can also be offered to children who are usually settled and happy at school but are dealing with a change of circumstance at home such as moving house or the arrival of a new baby. The additional comfort offered by the object may help them to adjust to the change more easily and manage their feelings of fear and anxiety.

The cycle of misunderstanding

Case study

Clare, aged 7, always pushed her way to the front of the dinner queue, knocking other children out of the way and hurting them in the process. This resulted in her being reprimanded, asked to apologise and spending lunchtimes on her own as the other children avoided her. Clare's behaviour resulted in her not getting any of her needs met as she had to go to the back of the line and wait even longer for her lunch. She felt lonely and sad as the other children refused to play with her. Clare was telling herself she was a bad person as the teacher had reprimanded her, and therefore she assumed that the teacher didn't like her.

Possible reasons for Clare's behaviour:

- She never had breakfast at home as things were chaotic.
- She panicked that there wouldn't be enough food for her if she wasn't at the front of the line.

- She was so overwhelmed by her hunger as she hadn't eaten that she had no awareness of the other children.
- She wasn't able to say that she was really hungry and was terrified that she may have to go without food.

How often in schools do we see scenarios like this where children are trying to show us what they need or how they feel and they are misunderstood and they get the opposite of what they need? The cycle of misunderstanding demonstrates an all too common scenario in schools.

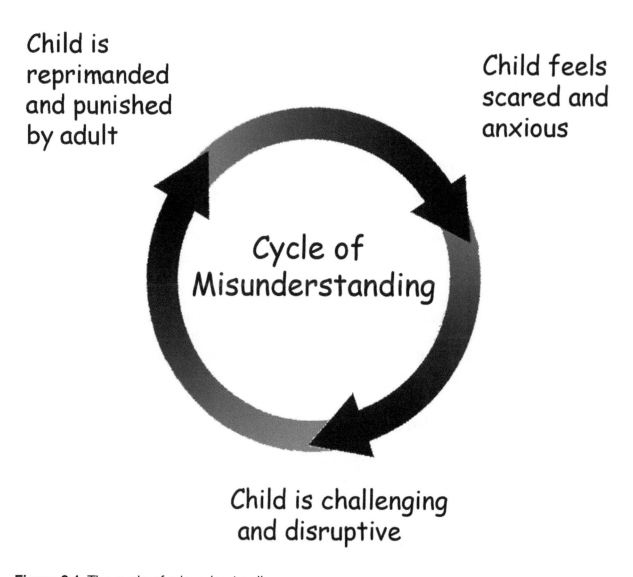

Figure 3.1 The cycle of misunderstanding

However, as has been discussed previously, for some children the contrast between behavioural expectations at home and school is huge. The conflict between acceptable behaviour at school is incompatible with acceptable behaviour at home. The norms of behaviour and morality that are developed at home can be poles apart from what is required at school and many children struggle hugely with this, only to be left with a sense of alienation as they get it wrong once again.

Children learn to develop their own coping strategies to manage their anxiety and this can manifest in different ways, from being disruptive and aggressive to being withdrawn and shutdown. It can be a challenge for school staff to try and work out what are the possible reasons for the child's behaviour, as well as trying to work out the best way to deal with it. The child's behaviour can often result in an outcome that increases their anxiety rather than reduces it. It can be useful to consider where the child is emotionally rather than developmentally as this can help to understand some of their behaviour, which may be more appropriate for a child of a younger age.

Table 3.3 What is this behaviour telling us?

Behaviour	What the child has learnt
Class clown	I need to get people to notice me and make them laugh and use humour to get them to like me
Bossy	I need to control things such as people, objects and tasks in order to feel safe
Perfectionist	I need to get things right, it's not ok to make mistakes and I need to do things in a particular way to feel safe
Bully	I need to make other people feel bad in order to make myself feel better because I think I am a bad person
Disengaged	Being in my own head and in my own world is familiar and the safest place to be
Fidgety	Fiddling with things helps me to feel safe and I feel scared and anxious when I can't do this

The examples above provide possible reasons why children have learnt particular behaviours as coping strategies to deal with their feelings. If a child needs to have an object to play with or brings in an object from home, it enables school staff to develop a greater understanding of how the child feels. Children who bring in objects from home may be telling us they need help to feel safe at school. If a child was able to put those feelings into words, it would be easier for adults to empathise and support them.

Case study

Kane, aged 6, had frequent tantrums in class if he couldn't get his own way. He would snap pencils and damage other equipment, attacking other children verbally and destroying his own work. After the tantrums he would sit with his head in his hands and sob.

Possible reasons for Kane's behaviour:

- He had witnessed domestic violence between his parents for the first four years of his life, resulting in him operating at an emotionally younger age.
- He felt scared and unsafe if he wasn't in control.
- He had learnt to use controlling and bullying as a way to manage his anxiety.
- He felt so awful about himself that he sabotaged his own work.

Kane's teacher was encouraged to reflect on the possible reasons behind the behaviour while maintaining clear and firm boundaries with him: 'I can see that you are getting really cross, you look furious, but it's not ok to hurt other people. We need to find another way for you to have your feelings and not hurt anyone.' This response provides a clear message to Kane that he is important. The teacher is validating rather than dismissing his feelings and is offering him support with expressing them, therefore breaking the cycle of misunderstanding.

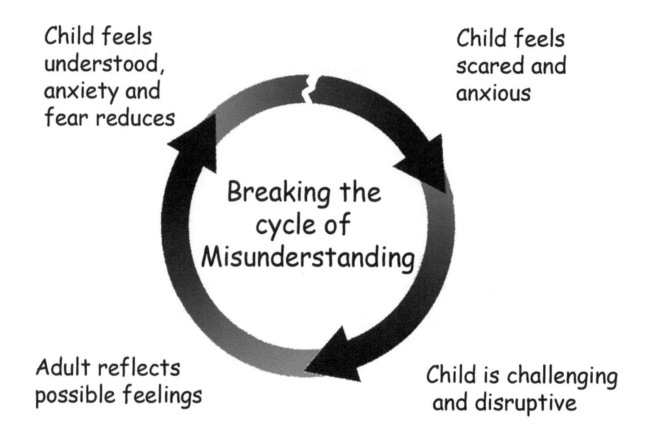

Figure 3.2 Breaking the cycle of misunderstanding

Using reflective language

Throughout this chapter and the rest of the book I provide examples of ways of using reflective language. Reflective language conveys to the child that you are seeing them, trying to understand them and acknowledging any feelings they may be experiencing. It enables adults to tentatively explore the child's experience without making judgements or assumptions about it. Using reflective language clearly communicates to a child 'I see you, I hear you, I am trying to understand you', and enables them to feel seen, heard, valued and understood. For some children this can be a relatively new experience for them and may result in increased self-worth and self-esteem.

Reflective language is a core concept of the group work programme and is key to its success. By using this with children, adults are providing a positive message to them: 'You are worth thinking about and trying to understand, I am trying to help you to work out how you feel and support you with understanding and managing your feelings.' It can be beneficial to use reflective language rather than always reprimanding children or telling them what to do, because it acknowledges and validates the child's feelings and experiences.

Case study

Tyreece, aged 7, was very disruptive during the first session of the friendship group. The facilitator explained that he kept going under the table and trying to make the other children laugh. She was feeling very anxious and finding his behaviour hard to manage. She was unsure whether to include him in the group for the next session.

Possible reasons for Tyreece's behaviour:

- His home life was unpredictable with no structure or routine.
- He had moved school three times.
- His class teacher was on long-term sick leave.
- He wasn't able to say that he felt scared and anxious when he didn't know what was going to happen next.

I encouraged the teaching assistant to talk to Tyreece before the group the following week as I felt he was probably very anxious. I suggested she offer him the chance to sit next to her for the rest of the sessions. I encouraged her to acknowledge how hard it can be when you don't know what is going to happen and to reflect: 'I can see that it's really difficult for you to sit still and relax until you know what we are going to do.' This reflection gave a strong and positive message to Tyreece that he was worth thinking about and trying to understand. I suggested she talk to him each week before the session and acknowledge his feelings and remind him that she would be there to help him with them. Tyreece responded well to this and relaxed as the sessions progressed. I encouraged the teaching assistant to share the process with his class teacher to raise her awareness of how he may behave when he is feeling anxious.

Children who find it difficult to show their feelings

This can occur when children have learnt to internalise rather than externalise their feelings. It can make it more difficult for them to cope at school and to build friendships. They may present as quiet and withdrawn or uncaring and find it hard to show any emotion. Their facial expression may remain the same throughout the day as the events and circumstances around them change; for example, a child who shows no remorse when they have hurt another child and appears to have no understanding of other people's feelings. It can be very difficult for a child to understand other people's feelings if they have little or no understanding of their own.

A child who finds it hard to show feelings may also have learnt to bury their physical pain along with their emotional discomfort. They may have learnt that no matter how much something hurts it is not safe to make a fuss or ask for help.

Children who feel unsafe

In order for children to achieve any success at school they need to feel both physically and emotionally safe. While this is essential for any child, if a child experiences their world outside of school as unsafe they may be vigilantly looking for evidence that the same is true at school. They may present at school as children who are eager to please and are constantly trying to work out what to do and what to say in order to get it right and please other people. In class they may be noticeable for their attentiveness as they can often be watching everything that is happening. They may be the last person to carry out an instruction because they are watching what everyone else is doing first in order to make sure they get it right and to ensure that the adult meant what they said. For example, the class are asked to go to their drawer and get their reading book. The child who feels unsafe may still be stood at their drawer looking at everyone else while the rest of the class are absorbed in reading. This child needs support with this and is not deliberately being slow or difficult. They are communicating their need to check things out all the time and a gentle reminder of what they need to do can help with their anxiety about this; for example, 'I can see you are stood by your drawer Joel and checking to see what everyone is doing, remember to get your book out and go to your seat then I'll come over and help you find the page.'

Staff strategy – to help a child who can't retain instructions

Give children one instruction at a time and praise them after each one to help them manage their anxiety about forgetting.

This type of behaviour can also be common in children that are so scared and anxious that they are unable to retain much information in their head. This may present itself as a child that is in their own world, not listening and disengaged. They may have their own anxiety-filled internal dialogue in their head, which may be punctuated with lots of terrifying 'what if' scenarios. The life experiences for children who demonstrate this behaviour may have been filled with real terrifying scenarios and so their experience of the world is that awful things are always happening. You may get glimpses of a child's anxieties, especially around periods of change. For example, on the day of the school trip they ask what will happen if the coach doesn't turn up or the zoo is closed. This snapshot into their internal world can help us understand how unsafe they feel and understand their experiences of good things going wrong. They need to be met with patience, support, understanding and reassurance to help contain some of their feelings for them.

Some children appear to be well behaved and compliant and may have developed this approach as a way of avoiding disapproval. For these children, the thought of upsetting other people is terrifying and they have learnt to ignore or bury their needs and please others first. They can appear to be extremely well behaved and 'no trouble' at school. They may feel that other people would not like them if they showed their true selves, so present a way of behaving that they think other people will like and approve of. These children benefit greatly from being involved in the group work programmes where all aspects of who they are is validated and accepted.

Children who display controlling behaviour

The reasons why a child may display controlling behaviour are many and varied. A child who bullies other children may be being bullied, dominated and controlled at home. They may be witnessing behaviour outside of school that demonstrates to them how to control and manipulate other people. For example, a child who has controlling parents who do not allow the child to make any decisions, or to have any choice or control over anything in their life, may also demonstrate this behaviour at school. A child who bullies other children needs help to find other ways to feel powerful and good about themselves. It is useful to explore how the child may feel about themselves as children with confidence and self-esteem who feel good about themselves do not need or want to bully other children.

Staff strategy – book of achievements

Divide the class list in to five days of the week and tell the children you are going to ask them to share something they have achieved or tried to do on their allocated day. At the end of the day before the class leaves, ask the chosen five or six children to tell the rest of the class and ask the class to applaud. Ask them to write or draw it in their book of achievements and each child will have approximately 38 by the end of the year.

Children who demonstrate controlling behaviour towards other children, such as trying to turn other children against them or manipulating them in to doing what they want them to, need the opportunity to experience success in other more positive ways. Children bring their own experiences of success and failure, fairness and justice with them to school, and depending on how these match the school experience may impact on their behaviour. When a child experiences conflict between these two experiences from home and school it can make it very hard for them to manage the differences and this is explored in more detail in Chapter Two. If a child is constantly challenging school staff it is an indication that they need help to build and sustain relationships. This is discussed in more detail in Chapter Five.

Children who have difficulty communicating

When a child finds it hard to communicate they need additional support to articulate their needs. If a child has English as a second language or is a selective mute, it is essential they are provided with the tools to help them to express their thoughts, needs and feelings. From the child's perspective, school life may be very frightening and confusing and these feelings may manifest in their behaviour. If a child chooses not to speak at school it is important to work on helping to reduce their anxiety rather than focusing on how to get them to talk.

Staff strategy – helping a child who chooses not to speak at school

- Offer them a notepad to draw in if they want to communicate with you; this can feel less intimidating than face-to-face conversations.
- Explore using picture cards to help them communicate their needs; e.g., water bottle, toilet, etc.
- Encourage them to choose a job to do in class with another child to help build relationships with other children.

Children who need help managing their feelings

When children are having tantrums and are raging, their bodies are having a physical response, which can exacerbate the situation if it is not responded to appropriately by an adult. Some children fight with others or throw things when they are anxious or scared; others will try and hide or run off. The reactions can either be fight, wanting to fight against the feelings and bodily sensations or flight, wanting to run away from them. Children who run out of class and/or hide around school are clearly communicating that they need help with their feelings. They may be saying 'I feel overwhelmed, terrified and unsafe and I need help to stop feeling like this.' If we respond to this behaviour by bringing the child back to class without helping them with their feelings, we are almost guaranteed that things will deteriorate as the day goes on. A response such as 'It's a shame you did that, how can I help you to make a different choice?' may diffuse the situation more easily.

Case study

Jacob, aged 5, was leaving his class several times a day. He was so adept at doing it that his teacher sometimes didn't notice as he would sneak out when she was using the whiteboard or crawl along the floor if she was working with a group. At other times he would just run. He had a variety of hiding places in his large school, which was an old building with plenty of space. The school staff would often spend a long time looking for him.

Possible reasons for Jacob's behaviour:

- He had moved house and school four times and found school work difficult.
- He felt overwhelmed and scared he would be in trouble if he couldn't do something so wanted to escape from his feelings of anxiety and fear.
- He had witnessed domestic violence at home and was used to making a den under his bed for him and his younger brother to hide in when they felt unsafe.

If a child is finding it difficult to stay in class it can help to create a den or calm space for them to go to in the class. This enables them to gradually be able to regulate their feelings and to enable them to access their learning again when they feel calmer and safer. There may be concerns from school staff that all the children in the class will want to go in the den, or that the child will want to sit in there all day and use it as an excuse not to do their work. However, in my experience this is not the case and rules for the use of the space can be agreed with the child. The situation can be used as an opportunity to explore the differences that exist in the class and to discuss situations that children may need help with. For example, 'Some children go out every day with Miss Giles to have extra help with their numeracy and other children need help with different things. The calm space is to help Jacob to have some time out when he needs it and we can all help him with this. Jacob is an important person in our class and we want to make it easier for him to stay in our class all day. Remember, in this class we are really good at helping each other with things.'

When a child has had help managing their feelings and some time out to calm down, they may feel safer and be able to access their learning again, rather than their anxiety and fear increasing and their behaviour deteriorating. It is a huge challenge to expect a child who has left the class to just walk in and return to their learning without any help or support from an adult. If an adult walked out of work or left a training course because they were upset, it would be extremely hard for them to just walk back in and carry on as though nothing had happened.

Staff strategy – creating a calm space in the class room

Ideally this will be a small area against a wall in a corner of the room, with cushions on the floor and a bookcase or table to create a sense of it being separate from the class and enclosed. It can have a sand timer, soft toys and a snowstorm or other soothing objects.

Explain to the child that you are going to make an area in class for them to help them when things feel difficult or scary. Ask if they would like to help you make it and talk to them about how they can use it. For example, 'I know that sometimes it can be very hard for you when we are doing our writing and it may make you feel anxious and scared. This is a place you can come to when you have those feelings and then me or Mr Clark will come and see if we can help you. This may help to make it easier for you to stay in the class with us and we'd all like it if that happened.'

You can set rules around the amount of time and how it can be used with the individual child according to their needs.

Children who have difficulty regulating stress may find it hard to tolerate excitement, resulting in them sabotaging events such as a school trip or Christmas party. In order to help children with this it is necessary to understand the feelings behind the behaviour. A child who associates Christmas or parties as a time that starts off happy but often ends in disaster may find it impossible to believe the experience will be any different at school. If a child is clearly showing that they are trying to destroy an event it is useful to ask them to do a job or offer the opportunity to help in a nursery or reception class with younger children while the preparations are taking place. This can help to manage their anxieties and ensure they do not create a situation that results in them missing the event due to their behaviour. These children need to experience positive examples of events that they associate with negative outcomes to provide them with alternative evidence and experiences.

During the group work training I deliver I encourage staff to think about the reason and the feeling behind the behaviour. When an adult is able to stop and think about the reason for the child's behaviour and what they may be feeling, instead of reacting instantly and making assumptions they are beginning to put the child and their emotional needs first. By tentatively reflecting and commenting on what they are observing, the adult is providing a powerful message to the child about the validity of their feelings and opening up opportunities for exploring alternative ways of dealing with them. The group work programme in this book provides a structured way for school staff to be able to integrate this into their way of working with children.

4 Integrating emotional well-being into the whole school

In the previous chapters I have discussed the importance of consistency in helping a child to develop emotionally and feel safe and secure at school. In order to be most effective, this consistent approach involves the whole school, is integrated into the curriculum and includes all staff from lunchtime organisers to head teachers. A whole school approach to emotional health and well-being is a key component of achieving success for individual children within the school. When considering the emotional health and well-being approach that a school is going to use, it is essential for the head teacher to ensure it can be filtered easily across the school and embedded into the ethos.

Whole school approach

In order to identify the success of a school it is useful to explore if the children are happy, settled and achieving their full potential, along with identifying any barriers to being able to achieve this. Throughout their day at school children are expected to deal with a variety of challenges such as trying new things, separating from their parent, etc. The way the school responds to the children's reactions to these events can influence their outcome. The school day is full of experiences that may evoke a range of different feelings in children and expose them to new and difficult situations. We may expect children to manage these without showing any response or reaction and may be surprised when they do. Children's fears need to be listened to and validated so they feel safe enough to voice them. School staff can develop self-awareness to ensure they are not being dismissive by using phrases such as 'don't be silly'. This can be discounting of the child's feelings and can exacerbate the child's fears.

The way that school staff respond to children showing their feelings has a big impact on their ability to understand and express them in a healthy way. It is important to consider how much the school accepts and encourages the expression of all feelings so children receive the message 'all feelings are ok', otherwise children may believe that it is not appropriate to show they feel sad, angry or cross. They may think that it is not acceptable to have or express painful feelings, only happy ones. Children need help with all their feelings from adults they can trust and feel safe with, so they are able to understand them and don't feel overwhelmed.

Table 4.1 Potential emotional impact of the school day

Situation	Feeling
Leave their parent	Scared
Follow rules	Overwhelmed
Listen to instructions	Confused
Manage changes such as having a new teacher	Terrifying
Eat lunch in a large hall	Intimidating

The messages that children receive from the school environment and school staff can also reinforce how they view themselves and how they experience the world. These experiences can provide subtle messages about issues such as trust and responsibility by small everyday tasks. For example, if a child is asked to deliver a note to another teacher they are given the message 'I can trust you' and 'You can be responsible'.

Making assumptions

Schools have a commitment to assessing each child's literacy and numeracy levels and providing additional support through interventions such as booster groups for children who may need it. However, in terms of social and emotional development they do not assess a child's social skills, but may sometimes reprimand them if they have difficulty in this area. We may expect children to be at a certain developmental level and make assessments based on their chronological rather than social and emotional age. For example, a 7-year-old who finds it difficult to share with others may be operating at an emotional level of a 3-year-old. It can be useful to consider the social and emotional skills that we may assume children have as we may think they are able to share, listen, cooperate, sit quietly, sit still, work with others and follow instructions. We can make assumptions that a child's age and developmental level are linked and for some children there can be a big gap in this being a reality. It is crucial that children are not punished for their developmental difficulties, i.e. not being able to share, but instead are provided with opportunities to practise and develop those skills as they would be with other areas of their development, rather than chastising them for not being able to do things. Does your school provide extra help and support in some areas, yet punish or reprimand children for not having the skills we expect them to have in others?

Staff strategy – visual reminders

If a child finds it difficult to share, take turns, be patient, etc. with other children, take photos of them doing this and create a book. Use it daily to remind them of the expected behaviour and how they have achieved it. For example, 'This is me sharing the Lego', 'This is me waiting in the line'.

This book can be used to reinforce the behaviour you would like them to do; for example, 'I remember when you were really good at sharing, let's have a look at that photo again.'

School staff may also presume that a child has a level of language and a cognitive understanding of the meaning of certain words. For some children, skills such as empathy and consideration are difficult to understand and even harder to put into practice. When children are operating at a much younger age in terms of their social and emotional development, they require extra support and clear explanations to enable them to achieve this. The group work programmes in this book can be used to enable children who need extra support to develop a range of age appropriate behaviour.

Opportunities in the school day

Throughout the course of a school day there are many situations that may enable children to feel good about themselves and to achieve success. These opportunities may need to be adapted to enable every child to experience positive results, just as we are able to differentiate a child's learning to achieve this. An example of this can be a 'Star of the day award' that can be presented to a child in class at the end of each day. This is an excellent way to ensure that every child receives this award at some point as it can be given for effort made, being kind, etc. rather than achieving a specific goal. There are also opportunities at school for children to experience disappointment and failure and for school staff to help them with the feelings these situations may evoke. This is an important aspect of developing resilience. The task of all adults in school is to acknowledge these feelings as they occur and help the child to manage them. It is important not to let a child win a game every time they play with an adult as this is unrealistic and will not build resilience. It is far better to help the child understand that everyone wins and loses at times and to help them explore and express their feelings about this. This can help them to develop persistence, determination and motivation rather than feeling overwhelmed and devastated. As discussed in previous chapters, this can be easier for some children to achieve due to their life experiences, and an individual needs-led approach can support this process.

Lunchtime

Lunchtimes in schools can be the most challenging part of the day, especially if the weather results in children having to be kept inside. The lunch period can be a difficult time for children as it is generally less structured and may feel disorganised and chaotic. This can be especially hard for children whose home lives may mirror this. The most effective way of managing this situation is to link a lunchtime organiser with each class who will ideally follow that class through the school, so there is some consistency of staff for the children. This can be difficult to implement as the lunchtime staff team may change frequently as staff leave the school. However, the more that all school staff feel they are an essential part of the school, and have the opportunity to have their thoughts and feelings listened to, the more likely they are to continue working at the school. It is essential that all staff feel valued and appreciated in their role, including the lunchtime staff.

They also need opportunities to develop skills and expertise and to be provided with guidance and support. A large amount of the afternoon session in school can be spent sorting out incidents that have happened over the lunchtime. This can be drastically reduced by equipping the lunchtime staff with support and the tools to understand and manage behaviour. Staff can often focus on telling children what they do not want them to do, rather than making it clear what they should be doing. Instead, try replacing don't with do and see if it makes a difference.

Staff strategy for lunchtime organisers

As a staff team, work in pairs and compile a list of examples of behaviour that you may ask children not to do; e.g., 'Don't push when you are in the dinner queue.' Change each example into the behaviour you would like to see.

Don't	Do
Don't push when you are in the dinner queue	Thank you for lining up nicely

Compile a list of the behaviour you would like to see and ensure you all use it each day to provide consistency across the school. Meet with the team again and review if you have noticed a difference in the children's behaviour.

Managing changes in the school day

As mentioned in previous chapters, the experience of consistency and predictability is essential for children's emotional well-being. Class teachers can contribute to this by acknowledging any changes throughout the day; for example, ensuring their class know when they are having their preparation time during the week. This can be helped further if the teacher returns to class afterwards to say goodbye to the children at the end of the day. This may result in the class being able to manage their teacher's absence more easily, and improved behaviour, knowing they will be returning at the end of the day to check on the class and review the afternoon. It is also possible for schools to use a similar approach when they are employing a supply teacher for the day. For example, the class teacher could leave a note to be read to the class at the start of the day. This would enable the class to manage their feelings more easily and provide a sense of predictability for them.

Dear Class Two,

Remember that I am on a course today to learn more exciting ways that I can help you with your reading. I will be back in class tomorrow morning and look forward to seeing you all then. I hope you all have a good day and show your supply teacher what a great class you are.

Mrs Omoboye

In order to ensure there is a consistent approach to behaviour and class expectations, any supply staff that are covering staff absences can also be provided with guidelines to manage behaviour. A supply teacher who manages behaviour by intimidating children or shouting can undo the ethos the school is trying to create. For example, 'In this school we encourage positive behaviour by acknowledging and praising the behaviour we would like to see increasing and find it helps the children if all staff use a calm, clear voice rather than shouting.'

Transition

As discussed in previous chapters, some children find any change extremely difficult as it can evoke feelings of loss, anxiety and uncertainty. It is useful therefore that children's transitions to new classes are managed with patience and understanding. For a child who has experienced many changes and uncertainty in their life outside of school, the transition to a new class and new teacher can be overwhelming. Children have to adapt to a new relationship, maybe a different way of working and a new classroom environment, all at the end of spending six weeks away from school. This is especially relevant for children in Year 2 who will be moving into Key Stage 2 after the summer holiday. This may involve being in a classroom in another part of the building or upstairs.

Staff strategy – helping with transition

Identify the children in Year 2 who may need extra support with the move to Key Stage 2 and start preparing them for this after the May half-term. Provide weekly walks to the Key Stage 2 area and acknowledge any feelings this may evoke in them. For example, 'It can feel a bit difficult moving to another part of the school, but remember there will be lots of people to help you feel settled.' Identify and discuss any significant differences with moving from Key Stage 1 to Key Stage 2; for example, a different playground or a change of break or lunchtime to help them manage the changes more easily when they occur.

The above strategies can also be implemented with the whole class to ease transition.

The first two weeks of term can be very challenging for children and staff and an important time to focus on developing and building the new relationship. This enables them to feel safe and to relax and engage with their learning. If this is not prioritised it can be very difficult to retrace and rebuild this. It is important that this is a gradual process and that allowances are made for children who may have difficulty building a new relationship.

Staff strategy – making a connection

Provide an opportunity for each child to make an 'all about me' poster to be given to their new teacher before their new class transition day. Encourage them to write or draw things about themselves that they are happy for their new teacher to know. For example, 'I love bananas and my favourite colour is red.' Their new teacher can spend time with each child on that day and share their poster with them. This can be a good way of making an initial connection with each child in a relaxed way. As the focus is on the poster, it can help children who find new relationships frightening and overwhelming.

The role of school staff

A beneficial tool for all school staff is the ability to reflect on themselves and their practice in an honest and open manner and consider how it may feel to be a child in their school. In order for them to do this they need to feel safe and reassured that their observations will be heard and responded to in a supportive way. This can start with the head teacher and other senior members of staff and filter down the school to the lunchtime organisers and office staff. The relationships and professionalism between staff across the school can create either a supportive and effective team or a divided group of people who are all struggling to go to work every day.

Qualities to develop in all staff

- Are all staff approachable?
- Are they supportive to each other?
- Can they rely on each other?

- Do they work as a team or compete against each other?
- Are they open and receptive to change?
- Are they honest about themselves and their work?
- Do they maintain professionalism and confidentiality?
- Are they able to reflect and admit their mistakes?
- Are they motivated and committed to the children and the school?
- Do they model good working practice?
- Are they resilient?

Staff training

The experience of high quality inspirational training is of paramount importance for all staff in school and opportunities to access additional training relevant to their role need to be available to all staff. The impact of this experience can be filtered across the school and new ideas and initiatives may be met with excitement and enthusiasm. Staff can be supported with identifying relevant training by formal and informal discussions and feedback on their performance. I feel it is beneficial to give feedback to staff on their relationships with children, not just their performance during lesson observations, as this is such a crucial aspect of their role in school. The relationships between children and staff are discussed in more detail in Chapter Five.

Staff relationships

The quality of the relationships between staff in school impacts on their ability to work together effectively and to model positive relationships to the children. The relationship between the class teacher, teaching assistant and support workers in their class need to be harmonious to ensure they are able to work together effectively. The relationship between staff working in the same class needs to incorporate open and honest communication along with mutual respect and appreciation. This can be demonstrated in front of the children so they are able to experience the impact of relating to other people in this way. When children have experienced living with disharmony and conflict they are more receptive to noticing this in other relationships.

If the relationship between staff is one of mistrust, resentment and animosity then this may be witnessed by the children through verbal and non-verbal interactions. When a child feels there is conflict between staff they may become preoccupied with trying to resolve this, rather than engaging with their learning. This may occur if a child is familiar with playing the role of peace maker and negotiator at home. Some children are very tuned in to relationships and will recognise atmospheres and behaviours between staff that can make them worried and anxious. Children need school to be a haven where they feel safe and protected and any negative feelings between staff and a difficult atmosphere will prevent this from happening. There are opportunities to show children how to manage feelings and conflict between people through the relationships between all staff across the school.

Staff morale

Adults working in school need to feel valued and supported in their work in order to be productive, and the morale of the staff can impact on the children in a positive or negative way. All adults working in school have a responsibility to create a happy and relaxed atmosphere for children, or to decide what they can do to change it. Working in schools can be a demanding and exhausting but rewarding and enjoyable job. In order for staff to work most effectively and give their best to the children they need to feel happy, supported and fulfilled. It is important they feel they are making a difference and that they are an essential cog in the wheel of school life. The school needs to be emotionally safe for staff in order to be emotionally safe for children.

Supporting each other

When school staff are confronted with challenging and disruptive behaviour from children it can be difficult to remain calm, to stay focused on the child and not to feel upset and angry. There may be pressure to demonstrate they are able to manage the child's behaviour either by the expectations they put on themselves or real and imagined expectations from other members of staff. It is essential that staff support and encourage each other with this in order that the person dealing with the behaviour doesn't feel helpless and inadequate. When children feel hurt and upset and are unable to deal with their feelings they may target the person they are close to and feel safe with such as a teaching assistant or support worker. If this happens it is essential that staff feel they have support and guidance from other members of staff, along with space and time to think about the child and their needs. This can enable them to develop resilience so they are able to reflect on the situation without taking things personally and react appropriately in the best interests of the child.

Appropriate staff behaviour

As mentioned previously, the messages we are communicating to children as adults has a significant impact on them. When working in schools, it is necessary for staff to have awareness of how their behaviour may influence the children on a daily basis. Staff whose behaviour is loud and outgoing may unnerve and intimidate children who may easily experience adults as frightening and overwhelming. If staff constantly joke and laugh with children it is important to check that they understand when you are being serious. It is our job as adults to decide and implement the boundaries around this for children and not to reprimand them if they become over excited. Some children are overly aware of what adults are saying and doing and may look for hidden clues in people's behaviour. For example, 'Mr Graves looked cross this morning, I think it's because I didn't finish all my maths yesterday.' In reality, the teacher had just heard that the printer was broken.

Reflect: How do I behave?

- Are my interactions always appropriate?
- What is my tone of voice and facial expression communicating?
- Do I have consistent boundaries no matter how I am feeling?

All children react differently to shouting, and while this may get their attention immediately in some situations, it can also provide mixed messages to children. If we reprimand children for shouting, or ask them to speak nicely to each other and then children hear staff shouting, we are causing confusion. We are saying one behaviour is acceptable for adults but not for children. There are occasions when it may be necessary for an adult to raise their voice in school; for example, if a child is about to fall or hurt themselves. However, adults may use shouting as a way of trying to manage children's behaviour. For a child who has experienced domestic violence or lives in a family where shouting is used as a way of communicating, this can be a very frightening experience. The child may tune out and appear to not be listening but actually may be feeling scared and unsure what to do. This can create even more anxiety and stress for the child.

Managing feelings

The school setting provides an ideal situation to demonstrate how to express and manage feelings on a daily basis. Staff can model ways of expressing their own feelings, often without being aware of it. Staff who sulk, moan, patronise and humiliate other members of staff, parents and children are providing powerful messages about how to manage feelings. If schools have clear expectations about children's behaviour and what is acceptable and unacceptable, they need to ensure this is implemented at all times by all staff. For example, a child told me they had heard a teaching assistant swear when they had been asked to cover another class. The child asked me if they would get a verbal warning, i.e. the same consequence that would apply to a child in school. It is essential that schools provide a consistent message to everyone in school and are not contradictory in their approach.

The way that the school staff react to everyday situations provides an opportunity to model ways of dealing with feelings to children. For example, if a member of staff makes a mistake or breaks something, this can be used as an opportunity to acknowledge this happens to everyone and that it is an important part of life. It can offer the chance to explain that mistakes allow us to learn and try things, rather than covering it up so children may think that adults never make mistakes. Throughout the school day there are so many learning opportunities that are not part of the curriculum that can be used for children to learn invaluable life lessons. For example, do adults apologise to children, do they demonstrate the behaviour we want children to have? Do children feel that there is room for them to make mistakes and that they get praise for being brave and trying things?

As adults we all have a responsibility to help children to understand and express their feelings rather than feel scared or overwhelmed by them. There are endless opportunities for school staff to share their experiences of managing their own feelings throughout the day. If there is a commitment from all school staff to use emotional vocabulary and share experiences appropriately with children, this can result in children being able to mirror this behaviour. This can be achieved by acknowledging situations as they arise throughout the day; for example, 'When I try something new I can get a sick feeling in my stomach, I know this is fear and it can help me to talk to someone when I feel like this.' Making statements such as 'Everyone has difficult feelings sometimes and it can help to tell people when we feel like this' can contribute to children's awareness of themselves and other people.

Using reflective language

We can also provide positive messages to children in a subtle way throughout the school day by thinking about and commenting on what is happening by using reflective language to tentatively explore what a child may be experiencing. This has been discussed in more detail in Chapter Three.

Table 4.2 Impact of positive reflective responses

Reflective response	Message to child
I've been thinking about how hard it is for you to remember your PE kit	You are worth thinking about
I'm going to ask Mrs Jones to spend some time with you and teach you how to put your coat on, I can see it frustrates you when you try to do it	You are worth helping
It's important that everyone has a turn at being at the front of the line	Your needs matter
You looked sad when you didn't get chosen for the science club, I wonder if you'd like to choose a friend and help me unpack the new books	You are important

The examples of reflective language provided enable it to be integrated into the school day. For example, if a child is struggling or finding a task difficult, it can help to reflect 'It can be difficult when we get things wrong' or 'It can feel frustrating when we are trying to do something and we can't work out how to do it.' This enables the child to feel noticed and understood, along with helping them to identify how frustration feels. Over time this enables the child to link the feelings with the word and to make that connection themselves. This may result in them being able to use the word themselves when they next have that feeling. It assists enormously if school staff are able to use this as a way of commenting on their own feelings; for example, 'I felt sad when I was unwell and missed the school trip.' See Chapters Eleven and Twelve for more examples of using reflective language.

Using affirmative language

The use of language is an important aspect of the behaviour approach within school, and using affirmative language which focuses on the behaviour you want to see rather than the behaviour you don't is a beneficial approach. For example, 'Please walk down the corridor' rather than 'Don't run' will often be more effective. When we focus on the aspects of behaviour we don't want, then that is what we will see. Children just hear the word 'run' and it gives them an idea; in the same way as we may say to a toddler 'Don't touch the plug', they just hear the word plug and immediately head towards it.

This approach is useful for children who have poor self-regulation and impulse control and may find it extremely difficult to change their behaviour and not do things. For example, if at home a child has to interrupt other people and talk over them to be heard then it can be difficult not to act in the same way at school. A class teacher recently used the phrase 'Who's being rude' as a way of managing a classroom situation. The child who was talking went red and looked ashamed. A different response, such as 'Remember we all need to listen to each other', would not have targeted and shamed the child and may have achieved the same result in a less direct way.

Listening to children

It is useful to consider how much time is allocated to listening to children's thoughts, feelings and ideas during the school day and explore whether children feel safe enough to do this. It is beneficial to provide opportunities for children to do this throughout the school year and for their ideas to be acknowledged and responded to in a positive and accepting manner. Some children who frequently say 'I don't mind' may have learnt this as a way of dealing with being let down and disappointed. They may pretend they don't mind as they have learnt 'There is no point saying what I want because I won't get it. It's easier to pretend I don't mind then I don't have to feel disappointed or upset.' These children need regular opportunities to make choices, along with validation that their ideas and feelings matter and are important.

Integrating emotional vocabulary in the curriculum

During the school day children may be asked to experience situations that adults may not feel comfortable experiencing, such as being vulnerable and sharing things about themselves which adults may find difficult to do; for example, asking a child to identify things they struggle with or find difficult. In class, an adult may randomly choose a child to answer a question, thereby exposing them in a way we would be uncomfortable with as adults. How many of us have attended training where we would feel uncomfortable if the facilitator randomly singled us out to participate?

Reflect: Would this feel comfortable?

- What do we ask children to do?
- How may it feel for them?
- How would I feel if someone asked me to do this?
- How can we change this to make it feel easier and less intimidating for children?

There are many opportunities during the school day to introduce and familiarise children with emotional vocabulary. It is essential to use this as often as possible so it becomes a recognised way of interacting and avoids children being asked to do something without naming and explaining it. For example, if a child hits another child and is asked why they behaved in this way, it is not realistic to expect them to explain if they are not provided with the appropriate vocabulary to be able to do this. The school staff ensuring they use regular opportunities to introduce emotional vocabulary to children can assist them with this.

Choices and responsibility

In school, children are provided with opportunities to learn about making choices and taking responsibility. This has a positive impact on their confidence, self-esteem and self-worth. If children are given choices over small things throughout the day, such as choosing to write with a pen or pencil, they are able to understand that with every choice comes a consequence. For example, a child who chooses to write in pencil is able to erase a mistake, whereas a child who chooses to write in pen is unable to do this. This can help them to understand more easily about the consequences of other choices they may make, such as, choosing to hit someone has a consequence of missing out on playtime.

When we give a child a choice or responsibility we are saying:

- I trust you.
- Your views are important.
- Your needs matter.

Creating the right environment

The physical environment that is created in a school impacts on the emotional well-being of everyone who comes in to school. For children who experience disorganisation and unpredictability outside of school, the organised and ordered environment of school contributes to their sense of safety and well-being. Classrooms that are clean, tidy and enable children to find things easily, and have things in the same place so children can access them easily, provide a sense of stability in children's otherwise unstable lives. A child who returns to school after a chaotic and unstructured weekend can feel soothed by knowing the felt pens will be in the same place on Monday morning. The children can be encouraged to have responsibility for taking care of their class and this can involve a team work approach. A sense of ownership and pride can be encouraged across the school but specifically in relation to individual classes. It is important to involve children in this as it is their space and the more comfortable they feel the easier they will find it to engage with their learning.

Within each class the children can have responsibility for their classroom, which can be implemented by allocating children to certain areas of the class and compiling a tasks list; for example, tidying the book corner, etc. The children can be given choice over the area, which provides an opportunity to ask them for their ideas about their classroom environment. This can be used to talk about managing differences of opinion and compromise and how to use skills of negotiation. It gives children the message 'We care about our class and each other.' At the end of each half-term it can be useful to have a class discussion to review what is working well and why. This gives the children a voice and sense of ownership over their class, along with developing team work skills.

Feeling safe and secure at school

School staff may make assumptions and have their own ideas about children's understanding of safety, but it is important to clarify this with them. The staff can also lead by example through their own behaviour and by ensuring that clear explanations are offered to children. For example, if a child is running while holding a pair of scissors they need an example of the alternative behaviour you would like to see along with an explanation of why they need to change their behaviour, such as 'Please walk when you are carrying scissors because if you trip or fall you could hurt yourself and I don't want that to happen.' It is important to be aware of not making assumptions about children's understanding or awareness of safety because of their age. Some children have no sense of danger because they may never have been made aware of it. These children may look confused when explanations about safety are offered to them. By acknowledging that you don't want a child to hurt themselves or that you want to keep them safe may come as a surprise for some children who may be physically or emotionally hurt by adults outside of school.

Staff strategy – increasing awareness of safety

Take children for a safety walk around school and ask them to identify the dangers both inside and in the playground. This enables you to assess each child's awareness and understanding of safety. It may bring you some surprises.

Emotional safety

Schools can play an important role in promoting children's awareness of emotional safety by exploring how we behave towards other people and why. It is beneficial to discuss why we are kind and care for each other and identify the feelings this may evoke. Children need to trust that the adults in school will protect them from harm in order to feel emotionally safe at school. This can be achieved by a clear and consistent policy for dealing with bullying and ensuring it is implemented by all staff. Schooldays can be the best or worst days of our lives and some of this is affected by friendships and peer relationships. It is essential that all children across school understand that any form of bullying is not acceptable and that staff understand that children who bully need urgent help. This is discussed in more detail in Chapter Three and Chapter Five.

It can be useful to consider how your school responds to children who are late arriving at school. If a child is late to a primary school then it is not their fault, although some parents may try and convince you that it is. For a child who is late, the embarrassment and shame of having to walk into their class when the lesson has already started is enough for them to have to deal with. Imagine how we as adults feel if we are late for training or a conference and have to walk into a room. Consider how difficult this can be for children to manage, especially if it happens on a regular basis.

Case study

Kyle, aged 6, arrives 10 minutes late for school. He looks tired, anxious and dishevelled. There is a history of domestic violence in his family and his mum is finding it hard to cope with his three younger siblings.

Teacher A response:

'Oh you're late again, tuck your shirt in and get your reading book and catch up with the rest of the class.'

Teacher B response:

'Morning Kyle, it's nice to see you. I can see you look tired, are you ok? Here's your book, we're on page 3.'

The response of teacher B is far more likely to encourage and enable the child to settle and engage with their learning than the response of teacher A, which is likely to increase their levels of anxiety and stress. The teacher who responds to a child's lateness by trying to make the child feel welcome and part of the class, however frustrating it may be, will help the child to feel reassured and valued.

An environment where children feel safe enough to make mistakes and are supported to learn from them provides an excellent learning opportunity. However, if a child who accidentally breaks something is reprimanded and punished, they may not only be too scared to admit when they do this in the future and may learn 'It is not ok to make mistakes.' This may prevent them from trying in the future and evoke a sense of shame about their behaviour. If an adult responds with compassion rather than irritation a child learns that making mistakes and breaking things is a part of life.

Behaviour system

The school behaviour system provides the foundations of the school and is most effective when it is implemented consistently across the school in terms of expectations and responses to behaviour. Any inconsistencies between adults may make children feel scared and anxious, resulting in them being quiet and withdrawn or challenging and controlling. This requires a commitment of all staff and an understanding of the importance of this. The behaviour system needs to be clear and understandable by children across the school and the behavioural expectations for the school to be realistic and achievable by all the children to enable everyone to achieve success. It is useful to ask the children for feedback on their understanding of it and how it works to ensure it has been understood. For example, if a child is regularly having difficulty following a particular rule, encourage the class teacher or another adult in school to check their understanding of it.

Helping children to understand behavioural expectations

It is important not to make assumptions about a child's understanding of behaviour without assessing it, just as we would assess their literacy or numeracy. For example, if a school rule is 'We are kind and gentle with each other', it is important to give the children examples of how they can achieve this. Some of the expectations we have about children's behaviour in school may make it very difficult for them to achieve success. For example, during assembly children may be expected to sit on a sometimes cold, hard floor and are reprimanded for being unable to do this without fidgeting or moving about. Most adults would find this difficult, yet we expect children to manage it. There may be limited alternatives as there may not be enough chairs for children, but if staff can acknowledge that it's a difficult thing to do, they are at least validating the children's experience.

To create an effective school environment the following attributes are useful:

Table 4.3 Useful attributes

Staff need	Children need
Patience	Understanding
Encouragement	Nurturing
Motivation	Consistency
Determination	Support
Support	Praise
Commitment	Encouragement
Tolerance	Recognition

It is essential in schools that school staff attempt to explore why children are behaving in particular ways, what they may be trying to communicate, how they feel and what can be done to help them with this. The more that children can feel understood and supported in trying to change their behaviour, the increased likelihood there is that this will happen. Imagine as adults if no one ever tried to understand us or help us to make changes, how would that feel?

Using behaviour charts

Behaviour charts are an invaluable way of monitoring children's behaviour and providing them with targets to achieve. However, they are most effective when they enable children to achieve some degree of success and to see the immediate results of their efforts. It is unrealistic to give a child more than one target. In the same way as we would not expect an adult to stop smoking, take up running, go on a diet and stop drinking all at the same time, because it would be unrealistic to expect them to achieve and maintain it, we need to apply the same philosophy when setting targets for children. For example, an initial target of 'good listening' for a child can be extended to develop additional changes once the child has experienced success.

Involving parents

Parents play a vital role in the school, and for a child to reach their full potential it is essential that they are as involved as possible, have positive experiences of the school and feel valued and supported in their role. It is most effective for the child if the relationship between parents and school is a harmonious one. It is worthwhile to make parents aware of and explain any interventions that are being offered in school so they are able to use a similar approach with their child at home. For example, a parent whose child was involved in the group work friendship programme was able to support this work by encouraging the child to practise the skills at home alongside the group, therefore maximising the potential for change occurring. As the parents in the school became more aware of the group work programmes and their effectiveness, this resulted in increased numbers asking for their children to participate. See Part Two for more information on the group work programme.

Developing life skills

The school setting is the ideal place for children to learn about and practise developing essential life skills, and the opportunity to do this can be integrated into the school curriculum through lessons and activities. The possibilities to do this are enormous and enable staff to be creative in their approach along with providing a template for developing and managing relationships. Qualities such as honesty, tolerance, compassion, courage, patience, etc. can all be integrated into the curriculum and develop resilience and other skills. It is important not to make assumptions about the skills that a child may have as this will depend on their external experiences, as discussed in more detail in Chapter Two. Children can be helped with skills such as organisation by involving them in working with other children and planning an event such as an end of term party. This is also useful for children who find it hard to work with other people and may find it difficult not being the centre of attention. Working with an adult such as a teaching assistant or learning mentor around a task like this can enable children to develop these skills or expand on existing ones.

The group work programmes in this book provide an important part of an effective whole school approach by creating opportunities for children to have additional support with emotional and social skills along with validating and appreciating their individuality.

For the group work programmes to be most effective, they need to be part of a whole school approach that reinforces the skills and experiences for children and staff. For example, Monique, aged 7, found it difficult to keep friends and could be bossy and controlling towards other children. The facilitator met weekly with Monique's class teacher and the teaching assistant in her class, sharing the skills they had been practising in the session and encouraging them to help her practise these in class. This approach enabled them to encourage her to transfer these skills outside of the sessions and provide the additional support she needed. This resulted in her friendships and confidence and self-esteem improving as she felt better about herself. If the group facilitator can liaise regularly with the parents, head teacher, class teacher and other adults working with the children across the school to provide feedback on the child's behaviour and share information, then this enables it to be fully integrated across the school rather than seen as a tokenistic gesture that may be hard to sustain.

5   Developing positive and meaningful relationships at school

Early relational experiences

In order for children to be able to build relationships with other people it is necessary for them to have a template of how to do this. A child's first relationship is with their main caregiver and this is usually a mother, father, grandparent or other relative. The quality of this primary relationship can determine the standard of future relationships. Children who have experienced their first relationship with a parent or carer that is nurturing, supportive, consistent and loving are able to develop an internal feeling of safety and security. This experience enables the child to explore freely and have a natural curiosity and excitement about life. As their early needs for food and stimulation have been responded to and their early interactions through babbling and gurgling have been met with enthusiasm and delight, they learn that their needs are recognised and met and they are worth thinking about and caring for, resulting in high self-esteem. They may present in school as having the skills and ability to build and maintain relationships and respond positively to help and support with this when needed.

However, a child who has had an erratic, inconsistent and unpredictable experience of early relationships may find it more difficult to internalise a sense of safety and security and may experience relationships as frightening and unreliable. If a parent or carer is emotionally or physically unavailable to the child, perhaps rejecting their needs and ignoring them or pushing them away when they cry, the child learns that their needs are not worthwhile and that if you seek comfort from someone you may be rejected. They may present in school as being quiet, withdrawn and self-contained. 'He seems happy on his own' may be how this child is referred to. For these children, relationships are frightening and to be avoided wherever possible, even if it means missing out on positive experiences.

Children need to have positive experiences of separating from their main carer to be able to manage the school day and relationships that occur within the school setting with both adults and children. If a child has not had this positive experience, it is possible to repair some of this by providing consistent, predictable, positive nurturing relationships in school with school staff. This experience can transform a child's early relational experiences and provide them with a strong base from which to develop and grow.

Case study

Marcel, aged 7, finds it difficult to settle and engage with his learning for long periods of time during the school day. He can be restless and disruptive in class.

Possible reasons for Marcel's behaviour:

- His mum was hospitalised for several months after a car crash when he was three months old and he was looked after by several family members during this time.
- His mum then experienced long periods of depression and was often unable to look after him properly.

The school understand that Marcel needs some help to manage his behaviour in class and has made a learning mentor available for him to access extra relational support at the start of each lesson. Marcel walks from his class down the corridor and across the hall to the learning mentor's room where he shows her his work and she checks his understanding of it and offers support and encouragement to him. The physical walk enables him to absorb the positive feelings he has just experienced and motivates him to settle and engage with his learning again. This opportunity provided by the school enables Marcel to develop confidence, self-esteem and to have an experience of being given responsibility for himself and his behaviour as he is trusted to go to the room and back on his own. This provides him with an alternative relational experience to the one he has had from his mum and enables his class to continue their learning without regular disruption from him.

Being a parent can be extremely stressful and challenging at times, and some parents may have little or no experience of receiving positive parenting themselves. A parent or caregiver who is overwhelmed by their own needs or difficulties may find it hard to respond to their child's needs in a consistent and caring way. They may be trying to keep themselves physically and emotionally safe; for example, if they are experiencing domestic violence, and may be unable to meet the needs of their child. Children who have this early experience may respond by being clingy, watchful and mistrusting of people. They may present in school as being controlling and manipulative in order to manage their high levels of anxiety. They may often feel very scared but have learnt to hide this through aggressive behaviour towards other children and school staff. They may focus on objects rather than people as they are easier to predict and manage; for example, a child who always fiddles with bits of paper or seems to have an endless supply of items in their pocket. This child may need to have these in order to feel safe, secure and settled in school. It is important for staff working in schools to consider this when removing objects that may appear to be rubbish or to have no significance as they may be of crucial importance and represent security for the child.

Staff strategy – helping children to manage their anxiety

Give the child an object such as a plastic animal or finger puppet and explain this is for them to have with them if they need help to do their work or sit still. Explain that they can choose a name for it and it has to stay in school so they can make a bed for it in their tray or drawer if they would like to.

The above strategy has been successfully implemented in many schools and although there is often initial uncertainty from school staff about the child just playing with it and not concentrating, it has been proven that the opposite is true. The child having an object to hold at times during the day has helped to reduce their anxiety and therefore enabled them to concentrate and focus on their learning more easily.

Relational experiences within the family

The ideas discussed in Chapter Two, which explores the impact of the family on the child's ability to learn and succeed at school, examine in more detail the effect of these experiences on children. If a child's needs are considered and met consistently during childhood they have a different experience to a child who has not had this. If a child feels unconditionally loved and valued for who they are and the joy they bring to their parents/carers, it is easier for them to approach and cope with school life. If a child feels that they are loved conditionally depending on their behaviour or not at all because of their behaviour, their sense of being worthwhile, valued and bringing joy to other people may be an unfamiliar concept to them. As discussed previously, children initially develop core beliefs and ideas about themselves within the family and these are validated by the messages they receive about themselves.

Table 5.1 Development of core beliefs within the family

Core belief	Validated by
I'm not good enough	Frequent criticism
My needs don't matter	Parents needs always coming first
I'm not safe	Unpredictable and inconsistent parenting
I'm a bad person	Experiencing abuse/domestic violence

Some families may find it difficult to model positive relationships with each other or with people outside of the family. As the family is the child's first classroom, the concepts they learn and experiences of how relationships are made and sustained are of crucial importance. This can be a major conflict between home and school. When a child learns within the family that relationships are about power, control and manipulation, and are encouraged to fight verbally and physically to get their needs met, the school setting with its different set of relational expectations and rules can be a very confusing place.

When a child experiences their parents regularly arguing or fighting they may think it is their fault, that they are responsible and that somehow they need to try and do something to make it better. They may become preoccupied with this and have little or no time or space to engage with their learning or to develop friendships. Sometimes a child is constantly trying to repair their parents' relationship by their behaviour; for example, 'If I put all my toys away then Mum will be happy and won't shout at Dad when he comes home from the pub and tell him to move out.' This may result in them appearing disinterested at school as they are thinking of new ways to make things better at home. This can also occur for children who may have a parent who is depressed and although they are physically present may be 'emotionally absent' and find it hard to interact with or engage with their child. This behaviour may serve as a self-fulfilling prophecy for their internal script that is already telling them they are wrong and bad and things are their fault.

It is a challenge to encourage children to develop and implement the school's relationship system in a way that is not demonising or criticising the child's experience within their family. How do we manage this without giving the message that school is right and your family is wrong?

Case study

Malakai, aged 5, witnessed his mum and dad hitting each other whenever they were angry, which was frequently. He learnt and witnessed repeatedly that this is how to respond to conflict. The messages he received were that if someone says or does something that you do not like then you need to hit them. This was reinforced by his parents telling him he was soft if he didn't demonstrate this behaviour towards other children in the street.

At school Malakai was very confused. If he behaved in a way that his parents approved of and that pleased them, then he received disapproval and got in trouble at school. He was constantly having to juggle two conflicting ways of behaving and would just be getting used to this when there was a school holiday and he would have to start all over again.

Relational templates

The relationships that are demonstrated between the adults within the child's family provide powerful experiences of how to manage these outside of it. While children may not be able to differentiate between helpful and harmful responses to situations, they are reliant on adults to provide examples of this for them. The way that this is shown to children can either help or hinder their ability to build relationships themselves.

Reflect: What messages may be provided by the following situation?

A child witnesses their parents arguing and fighting. Mum tells Dad to leave and Mum gets a new boyfriend. Mum tries to stop Dad seeing the child as a way of punishing him. Dad refuses to give Mum any money until she lets him see the child and tries to phone the child to speak to them. Mum refuses to let the child speak to Dad or have any contact with him.

Messages to the child:

- Conflicts are not resolvable.
- Relationships are replaceable (mum gets new boyfriend).
- Relationships are about power and control.
- Relationships are not about compromise or negotiation.
- Relationships are confusing and unpredictable.
- My thoughts and feelings don't matter.

Children bring their templates of how to build and maintain relationships with them in to school. Each child already has countless examples of relationships they have experienced and witnessed by the time they come to school and their experiences at school can either reaffirm or challenge this.

Negative messages children may learn about relationships within the family:

- You have to fight for everything.
- Relationships are hard.
- Don't trust anyone.
- Everyone is out to get you.
- It's good to get one over on people.
- Having feelings is a weakness.
- It's good to hurt other people.
- Don't be vulnerable.

Within the family there are expectations that parents love each other and their children, but this can be difficult to do if a parent has not had this experience themselves and does not understand how to do this. The experience of how sibling relationships are established and managed within the family provides a useful opportunity for families to encourage children to practise and develop skills that will be beneficial at school and in the wider community. When children have had positive experiences of managing feelings of jealousy with siblings, along with dealing with conflict and competition in a positive way, this enables them to transfer these skills to experiences at school. The relational patterns that children are exposed to are internalised and may become a reality in school. Children develop their own internal guide to making friends and engaging in relationships with adults in school and this may manifest in their behaviour towards other people.

Table 5.2 What has this child been taught in their family?

Kindness	or	Hostility
Compassion		Humiliation
Respect		Degradation
Understanding		Hostility
Tolerance		Indifference
Acceptance		Rejection

Helping children to develop appropriate friendships

When children have had the experiences described, it is important that the school recognises that they may not have the social and emotional skills appropriate for their age. It is vital that each child is assessed for this rather than expecting them to automatically be able to manage relationships with children and school staff. It is crucial that they support children who do not have the skills to build and maintain friendships, rather than punish them for not having them.

The school setting provides the ideal situation for children to learn basic friendship skills and it is useful to explore opportunities within the school day and at after school activities to do this. Children who have friends feel happy, confident and good about themselves. They are more able to focus and engage with their learning rather than feeling worried and anxious about their lack of friends and how they feel about themselves. The school can support children who need additional help to build friendship skills by using a caring approach that is nurturing rather than punitive, which will achieve more positive results.

The group work programmes provide an opportunity for children to receive additional support with their social and emotional development and enables them to develop the necessary skills to manage relationships more successfully. The activities and tasks are devised to enable children to practise social skills such as sharing, compromising, negotiating, waiting for their turn, etc., which are skills that some children may not have had the opportunity to develop outside of school. The supportive environment created by the group facilitator enables children to experiment with behaving differently and taking a risk. For children who have no resilience, lack confidence and self-esteem and can't manage their peer relationships, the chance to practise these skills in a safe and supportive environment can help eliminate their feelings of vulnerability and isolation. The group can encourage children to have good feelings about themselves by providing messages such as 'You can contribute your ideas and do things well, people like you', which are all essential ingredients to enable children to build and sustain friendships. The sense of belonging created by being in the group on a weekly basis enables children to build an alliance with the others in the group and assists them in building friendships that may be transferred outside of the group.

The activities and tasks in the group work programmes enable children to develop positive feelings about themselves through their behaviour. For example, an activity making something for someone else (week three friendship programme) provides an opportunity to explore how this feels and why. This develops positive feelings and increases the likelihood of the behaviour being repeated outside of the group so children activate those feelings about themselves again. The development of these skills and the heightened awareness of other people enable friendship skills to be practised and implemented on a daily basis. For example, a child who was previously quiet and withdrawn may find his voice and start offering to help the class teacher more often. The benefits of the group work programmes are discussed in more detail in Chapter Seven.

Children who need help with friendships

There are a variety of reasons why some children find it more difficult to make friends and we have already explored some of these. When a child does not have the skills to make connections with other people they may use their behaviour as a way of getting a response and being noticed; for example, a child who pokes or prods another child to make a connection because they do not have the language or social skills to know where to begin. For children who find making and keeping friends difficult, it can reinforce their sense of loneliness and isolation when they can't seem to get it right in making connections with other children.

Case study

Jermaine, aged 5, found it difficult to make friends with the other children in his class. He would knock into them, push his way to the front of every line and snatch things if he wanted them. He was loud and controlling, constantly telling children to 'move' if they were in his way.

Jermaine's poor social skills, emotional vulnerability and challenging behaviour all resulted in him behaving at the developmental level of a child of a much younger age. The other children were afraid of him and avoided being near him whenever possible, which reinforced to him that they didn't like him. This downward spiral can be difficult to break without additional help, nurture and support in school.

Staff strategy – the book of kind things

For children such as Jermaine, devise 'Jermaine's book of kind things' and find one kind thing every day that he can do to help staff, children or around the school generally. At first they may need help identifying what they can do, but gradually encourage them to have their own ideas. Each day record this in their book, which they can decorate and keep in their drawer at school. Every Friday photocopy the week of kind things for them to take home.

This activity helps to identify positive aspects of the child and focuses on finding qualities they possess that may otherwise be overlooked due to their challenging behaviour. It builds their confidence and self-esteem as they start to feel better about themselves and realise what they have to offer. The responses from the other school staff and children help to support this and enable the child to be viewed in a more positive way. Gradually they are able to practise social skills once they feel more confident and have a stronger sense of self.

Reflect: Think of a child you know and consider the child's relational template

- What is this child's experience of relationships at home?
- What is this child's experience of relationships at school?
- What do they need?
- How can I help them with this?

Children who bully

Children who torment, intimidate, control or manipulate other children may be showing adults they desperately need help with their social and emotional skills. When a child displays any of these behaviours they are clearly communicating that they are unhappy and need help to feel better about themselves. Children who actively hurt others are often hurting themselves. Children who are happy and settled do not need to hurt other people.

Possible reasons for children bullying:

- low self-esteem;
- lack of confidence;
- negative sense of self such as 'I'm a bad person, I'm not good enough';
- being bullied themselves;
- being controlled outside of school so using control to feel powerful;
- lack of control and choices at home.

While it may be a challenge for school staff to look beyond the child's behaviour, this is the key to enabling them to change it. Children who display bullying behaviour need nurturing and to feel good about themselves.

Children who bully need:

- opportunities to develop personal strengths and qualities;
- to have choices and contribute to decision-making wherever possible;
- a positive relationship with an identified person who can get to know them and support them to get their needs met in more positive ways;
- school staff to show an interest in them and spend time getting to know them so they feel more positive about who they are.

Reflect: Dealing with bullies

- How does your school deal with children who bully?
- Does this activate more negative feelings and increase self-loathing for them?
- If so, how can this be changed?

Children who experienced multiple transitions

As mentioned in Chapter Two, children who have moved house and school several times in their lives may need extra support with friendships and adjusting to school life. They may require additional support settling in to the class and feeling comfortable at school. This can be achieved by providing additional adult help if it is available and preparing the class to welcome the newcomer. The experience of a new child starting in a class provides an ideal opportunity to work with the rest of the class to explore how this may feel and what they can do to help the child. It is a useful way to introduce concepts such as empathy, support, compassion, differences, etc. with the class and to enable them to practise and develop a new understanding and set of skills. The class teacher can consider the class environment and where the new child will sit, who can be a buddy to them and when and how this will be reviewed. If a new child is provided with a positive and welcoming start, this can help alleviate some anxieties the child may be feeling.

Children who experience many changes of school also need the opportunity to experience a positive ending from the school they are leaving, even if the staff are all breathing a sigh of relief. This can be achieved by allocating some time with a familiar member of school staff such as a teaching assistant who can take the child on a tour of school taking photos of them at various places such as the dining hall, playground, etc. and making a scrapbook with them. The rest of the class can spend this time making either an individual or a whole class card for them to take with them when they leave. Give a child a positive ending at your school so they can have a more positive beginning at their new school.

Consider your contribution

The vast majority of adults who choose to work in schools like working with children and enjoy their company. The key to any good relationship, including those between school staff and children, is the ability to self-reflect. This involves an honest appraisal of the following:

- What do I react to and why?
- What do I struggle with and why?
- What do I honestly think about children who show challenging behaviour and why?
- What do I honestly think about children who bully and why?
- What do I think about children who lie and why?
- What do I think about children who steal and why?
- What do I think about children who hit other children and adults and why?
- Am I as happy as I could be with the relationships I have with the children?
- What could I do to change this?

The more honest that school staff can be with themselves about the behaviours and relationships that they find difficult and why, the more they are able to change this and improve the relationship they have with the children in their school. It may be a complex and painful task to do this, but it can also be a liberating experience resulting in staff ensuring they do not punish children for their behaviour because of how they are feeling. Some children may evoke difficult feelings in adults and school staff may start behaving differently towards them; for example, if a child has been rude or disrespectful towards you it may be hard not to ignore them or be stricter with them the next time you see them.

It is essential that school staff look after and support each other's emotional well-being and are able to identify ways to manage their stress. Strategies such as going for a short walk around school, popping outside or having a cup of tea can all help to reduce the likelihood of stress levels increasing. School staff need to be able to look after and support themselves so they are able to look after and support the children. If staff are feeling fragile, stressed or vulnerable, this will impact on their ability to develop and maintain relationships with the children.

It is also useful if staff can separate the behaviour from the child and remember this is the way that the child is communicating; it is not a personal attack or a deliberate way of making your day more difficult. It is important that staff try and stay calm and model this for children and avoid getting into power struggles. If the adult is able to stay calm, this will help the child to regulate their own feelings. Explore what is motivating your response to a child and ensure you are responding in an adult way.

Table 5.3 The impact of using an alternative response

Child's behaviour	Adult's response	Child's behaviour
Child is angry and shouting (child feels scared and anxious and thinks 'You can't manage me and I don't feel safe')	Adult feels angry and shouts back (adult feels scared and anxious and thinks 'I can't manage you')	Child increases level of anger and shouts louder (child feels terrified and thinks 'I knew you couldn't manage me')
Child is angry and shouting (child feels scared and anxious and thinks 'You can't manage me and I don't feel safe')	Adult responds with calm and reassuring tone of voice (adult feels in control and thinks 'I can manage you')	Child feels understood, soothed and thinks 'I am beginning to feel safe again now'

If school staff are committed to having better relationships with children and are able to honestly reflect on the barriers that are preventing them from achieving this, then they have started on a journey to be able to achieve this. The following activity can be implemented using a class list every half-term and is a useful way to keep evaluating your relationships with the children.

Reflect: How well do I know my class?

Look at your class list and consider the following:

- How well do I know the children in my class?
- How do I manage my relationships with quieter/shy/less confident children?
- Can I identify the children who find it hard to ask for help?
- Which children do I have good relationships with and why?

Staff experiences

Each member of school staff will have their own story and experience of their own schooling that they bring with them to work every day. This may have been a positive or negative event and may impact on their present day experiences in school. It may affect the way they interact with the children, their beliefs about behaviour and how it should be responded to, along with how they feel about their job.

Reflect: How does your experience of school impact on your relationships with children and reactions to their behaviour?

Think of a child who you find challenging or difficult.

- What is it that you find difficult?
- Do they challenge you or undermine you?
- How does that make you feel?
- Why do you think they do this?
- What can you do to improve your relationship with that child?
- How would you feel if you achieved this?

Both school staff and children will bring experiences and ideas to the school setting each day. Children bring their own experiences of how behaviour is managed at home and in the wider community, along with attitudes to school and learning and an acceptable code of conduct they have learnt. Adults have their own experiences of early childhood programming that they carry with them into adulthood. School staff bring their own expectations about how behaviour should be managed, their own attitudes towards school and learning, along with an acceptable code of conduct they have learnt. The more compatible these are, the increased likelihood of successful relational experiences occurring for staff and children.

The quality of the staff and child relationship

The quality of the staff and child relationship affects the teacher both emotionally and professionally and the child in terms of outcome, achievement and positive sense of self. The staff perception of the child affects the relationship between them and the staff's efforts to engage and motivate the child. There are some children that it is very easy for school staff to have a good relationship with. These children are often confident, articulate and pleasant to spend time with but may also be quiet and eager to please. They are compliant and respond well to adult interactions and praise. However, it is the children that staff find most challenging and difficult to spend time with who need it the most. These children may present as antagonistic, argumentative and disrespectful. They may appear to have no interest in building relationships with school staff and seem to go out of their way to make school life as hard as possible for themselves and everyone around them. It is not surprising therefore that most school staff would not choose to actively try and develop a relationship with them.

Staff strategy – to help a child who finds it hard with new members of staff

Work with the child to create a 'getting to know me' information sheet. Include:

- Things I like . . .
- Things I do not like . . .
- I sometimes need help with . . .

When a child has a support worker working with them on an individual basis, the relationship between them can be very intense. It is sometimes the children that most need help with relationships, either with children or adults, that have support workers and this can contribute to the need for extra help and guidance for the member of staff working in this role in school. They play a valuable part in ensuring that children are able to reach their full potential, but the role is not without its difficulties. For example, a child may find it hard to settle and engage when the support worker is not there or may be jealous or find it hard to share them with other children in the class and across the school. It is crucial that their role is clearly explained to both the child and worker to ensure that these situations are easier to deal with. The school can offer support for the child around these changes and provide them with explanations and advance warning.

For example, a child could go to another class to work with a teacher they are familiar with if their support worker has to go to a meeting and they may find it difficult to manage their behaviour in class without them. This is a useful opportunity to make appropriate changes to meet the child's needs and is not rewarding the child for their behaviour. It is important this is explained to all school staff to ensure there is understanding across the staff team and to discuss why this change is being implemented.

Building relationships

It is worthwhile exploring what opportunities exist in school to build relationships between staff and children and how these can be increased. In the classroom there are situations that can be adapted to develop relationships more fully; for example, during bad weather and wet play where children are unable to go outside, or free choice time known as 'golden time' in some schools. While it may be tempting to spend this time marking or doing preparation, it can be a good time to develop relationships with the children and to see other aspects of their personalities in an informal, relaxed and fun way.

For some children, the experience of spending individual time with a member of school staff may seem terrifying. These children may have experienced adult relationships as being unpredictable and inconsistent and have developed this avoidance as a coping strategy and a way of feeling safe. They need to be able to experiment being in close proximity to an adult while still feeling safe and in control. A useful way to provide this can be to offer them the opportunity to choose a friend to do a job for you with them. This gives them permission to be as close or distant from you as they need to be. Gradually over time as they develop a relationship with you, they may become more relaxed and be able to initiate this for themselves. It is essential that they are encouraged to build the relationship themselves and that it is not rushed as this may result in them feeling anxious and overwhelmed. All school staff have a responsibility to consider children who have difficulty building relationships and identify who could be made available and what can be done to help them when they feel scared or anxious in order to help them feel safe and secure. If this is overlooked and not prioritised, it can seriously affect children's ability to fully engage with their learning. Positive relational experiences are a basic human need and should not be used as a punishment or a reward in our schools. A sense of security with an adult in school is essential to a child's social and emotional development and emotional well-being.

Staff strategy – have I encouraged the children I work with to feel good about themselves today?

- Have I praised them?
- Have I acknowledged positive behaviour?
- Have I identified helpful hands?
- Have I recognised both effort and achievement in children's work?

Staff leaving

When a member of school staff leaves the school either during or at the end of the school year, this can have a big impact on some children. It is important for schools to consider how this is communicated to the children and when they are told. Some children develop close relationships with school staff and are devastated when they leave. It can be a huge loss for them and needs to be managed with thought and sensitivity. Children need to be given plenty of notice rather than being told on the day the person is leaving. The ending needs to be marked in some way and the children offered the opportunity to make cards or draw pictures if they wish to. They need clear and honest explanations and the chance to ask questions in order to understand what is happening. When children have experienced adults coming in and out of their lives or just disappearing overnight due to relationship breakdown, it is essential that schools provide them with a supportive and reassuring experience of an ending with an adult.

How do children experience school staff?

As I discussed earlier in this chapter, each child brings their own template of relationships to school with them based on their experiences outside of school. The relationships with staff at school can provide an alternative template for some children. For children who have developed vigilance as a way of feeling safe, they may notice non-verbal as well as verbal responses to situations. For example, does a member of staff frequently stand with their arms folded or regularly frowns or looks cross? What may this communicate to a child? In order for school staff to develop positive relationships they need to be aware of the significance of every interaction with children.

Reflect: How approachable are you?

- Do you smile at children when you see them?
- Do you show children you can be trusted?
- Do you show interest in the children?
- Do you encourage children to talk to you if they want to?
- Do you listen when children talk to you?
- Do you support children with their feelings?

The acknowledgement of your role in school can also help to support this process; for example, offering help to a child by saying 'Sometimes adults can help you with things' or 'My job is to keep you safe' to a child who is being bullied. These responses are particularly important for children who have learnt self-sufficiency as a coping mechanism in order to feel safe. If staff listen to children's thoughts, ideas and opinions they feel listened to and valued and may be more inclined to repeat this behaviour. If a child lives with fear and anxiety they do not have inner peace and calm and may experience the world as unpredictable and dangerous. School staff may unconsciously reinforce this belief by responding in unpredictable and reactive ways to children. When school staff respond to children's anxieties and fears with compassion and understanding rather than dismissing them as silly or inconsequential, they are validating the child's experience and enabling them to feel safe and supported at school. The experience of fear is a natural developmental stage for 5–7 year olds who may think there are monsters under the bed or in the school cupboard. They need help from a caring adult to help them understand and express their feelings so they do not feel overwhelmed by them.

It is essential that staff take responsibility for and acknowledge their own mistakes and apologise when they get things wrong. We cannot expect children to do this if we are not able to do this as adults. The experience of making mistakes and getting things wrong without being shamed, humiliated or experiencing disapproval is a key factor in children being able to persevere and try again with tasks. This can be achieved by providing strong and consistent relational experiences with adults in school who can support and nurture them, along with adults modelling how they deal with making their own mistakes.

When children interrupt staff frequently and find it hard to wait to be listened to, this may be an indication they do not get heard at home. It is important to be aware of how children who interrupt are responded to in school; are they criticised or humiliated thereby evoking feelings of shame for the child, or responded to in an understanding way? It is very difficult for children (and some adults) to not say what comes into their head immediately. It is helpful and supportive to a child's confidence and self-esteem if they can be praised for being patient rather than penalised for being impatient.

During the group work programme I acknowledge a child interrupting by saying 'It's hard to wait when you have something you want to say, but try and remember it and I'll come back to you in a minute', or I focus on their ability to be patient by saying 'Well done for being so patient, that can be a hard thing to do.' These responses support the child in trying to change their behaviour rather than a punitive response which may make them feel uncomfortable.

When children feel that their opinion matters it enables them to formulate their own ideas, to make decisions and to value what they think. This is essential for the development of confidence and self-esteem and to cultivate a strong sense of self-worth. When children are encouraged to have dreams and aspirations and these are responded to in a positive way by school staff it provides a message of hope and conveys that things are achievable. This motivational response can help children to believe that things are possible and work to achieve them.

What are staff modelling by their relationships with each other?

Throughout the school day staff are interacting with each other and working together or alongside each other. School staff are provided with endless opportunities to model positive ways of interacting and demonstrate harmonious working relationships. It is useful to consider the relationships between staff and the messages they provide to the children; for example, does a child think 'Miss Jones must hate Mrs Sullivan, she's always moaning about her.' This response is not only unprofessional and inappropriate for a child to witness, it also communicates about how to manage conflict, i.e. just moan rather than talk to the person and try and work out what the problem is. Adults working with children have a responsibility to demonstrate appropriate ways of expressing and dealing with their own feelings; for example, sharing excitement about a school trip.

What message does the following behaviour communicate to children?

- Staff being negative about each other.
- Staff snapping at each other.
- Staff challenging each other in an aggressive manner.
- Staff asking each other for help.
- Staff providing help to each other.
- Staff supporting and encouraging each other.
- Staff being relaxed with each other.
- Staff respecting each other.

- Staff valuing each other's opinions.
- Staff communicating easily and clearly to each other.

Reflect: Do staff walk their talk?

Do school staff behave as they expect the children to?

When children are trying to navigate their way around their life at home with unpredictable and inconsistent parenting they do not have a map to help them make sense of it. At school they are provided with a clear map in terms of rules and boundaries, but may need additional help understanding and following it. The school staff's increased awareness of this need for some children enables them to provide opportunities to support them with this throughout the school day. If children feel happy, safe, settled, valued and secure in school then with the support of school staff they are able to be focused and ready to learn. They have the capacity to reach their full potential. How many children in your school feel like this every day and what can you do to improve it?

6 You can make a difference

The vital role that school staff play in contributing to children's emotional well-being cannot be underestimated and can be utilised more to ensure it is maximised to its full capacity. Every adult who works in a school has a responsibility to support children's emotional health and well-being and contribute to ensuring they feel good about themselves on a daily basis. The quality of the relationship between adults and children is crucial and every interaction can have a positive and meaningful outcome. As I discussed in Chapter Five, everything you say and do can affect children in either a positive or negative way; it can either enhance or erode their self-esteem and sense of self. We need to consider carefully what we say and how we say it, as this can have a big impact on a child. Our facial expression, body language and tone of voice all have meaning and will be interpreted by the child who is on the receiving end. This is of vital importance for children who are tuned in to adults' every move. They can be vigilant at trying to translate every movement and gesture, as well as the actual words that are spoken. When children have had negative experiences of how adults perceive them, they are especially competent at looking for evidence to validate this negative view of themselves. Mannerisms such as an adult waving their arms around, even in excitement, can cause anxiety and increase stress levels for children who live with unpredictability. The use of a gentle tone can go a long way in establishing a safe relationship for a child who is anxious and scared.

> ## Reflect: Think about the changes you can make
> - What can I do to make a difference to a child in school today?
> - Will this make a small difference to me but a big difference to a child?
> - How committed am I to making a difference to a child's life?

Try alternative ways to respond to children's behaviour

Throughout this book I have been encouraging school staff to try different strategies to deal with children's behaviour. It can be easy in life to keep doing things the way we've always done them and harder to be brave enough to experiment with another way. However, as has been discussed in the previous chapters, the significant relationships between school staff and children that can occur in school settings enable both children and staff to experiment with this concept. The more that school staff can get to know and understand the children in their care, the more they will be able to develop appropriate responses to behaviour to meet the child's needs.

Case study

Hannah, aged 6, found it very hard to sit on her chair. She would lean from side to side, sit up on her knees and rock on it, occasionally falling off.

Teacher response

Her class teacher understood that this was something that Hannah found difficult and needed help with and acknowledged this to her by saying 'I can see it's really hard for you to sit still on your chair, I'm wondering if we should spend some time together to see if I can help to make it easier for you.' The teacher spent time showing Hannah where to put her feet so they could be settled comfortably on the floor and explored with her how this felt.

Result

Hannah responded to this help from her teacher by becoming more aware of how she was sitting and with gentle reminders such as 'I'm wondering if you need a bit more help with your chair?' was able to manage sitting at the table more easily.

While this teacher response may not have had the same effect with other children, if school staff are able to think for a minute before responding to behaviour, they may be able to adapt their responses to meet the child's individual needs. This may result in the child feeling more understood and have a positive outcome for both staff and child.

Focus on behavioural expectations

Sometimes addressing the class as a whole or wondering aloud can be a useful way of supporting individual children to try and change their behaviour and can be less punitive than targeting individual children. For example, when the noise in the class is increasing it can be helpful to acknowledge this by saying 'It's quite noisy and I'm just trying to work out where the noise is coming from' or 'The volume has gone up again, can we all try and get the volume down again please.' Both suggestions are clearly communicating a behavioural expectation for the whole class and provide gentle ways of helping children to achieve this. The behavioural change can then be acknowledged and praised, such as 'That's much better, well done for making the change I asked for.' When all children are clear about the behavioural expectations that school staff have of them, it may make it easier for them to work together and support one another in achieving this. The focus and validation of the behaviour that you would like to see, rather than the behaviour that you don't, provides a positive reinforcement to all children. This is particularly important for children who have the opposite experience of this outside of school, as they are able to achieve a level of success and sense of accomplishment in school increasing the desire for them to repeat this behaviour.

Staff strategy – to help engage the whole class

'Who can I see that looks ready to listen? Who can I see that looks ready for learning?'

This strategy is a gentle way of reminding the class of a behavioural expectation you have of them giving you their attention when you ask for it.

Spend extra time with children

Investing just five minutes a day with a child can have a huge impact. I have encouraged school staff to do this at lunchtime while they are clearing up or setting out the class and it has provided children with a different experience of a staff relationship. The child can be involved in sharpening pencils or putting out books and it enables an informal interaction to take place and the relationship to develop. The message it gives to children is positive as it validates who they are. In previous chapters I have discussed the importance of this and how it can enable their internal dialogue to be rewritten; for example, 'If Mr Malik has chosen me to do an important job for him at lunchtime then maybe I am not a bad person.' The outcome for the child is beneficial in terms of relationship experience and developing confidence and self-esteem. The sense of purpose and importance developed by offering children the opportunity to help with jobs enables them to feel better about themselves. However, a note of caution is necessary to ensure that children do not feel they are only of value or importance when they are helping other people, so this needs to be considered when identifying children who may benefit from this additional input.

Reflect: What do I do?

- How often do I show interest in the children?
- Do I remember things they tell me?
- Do I remember to ask them about things they have told me?

Be a significant adult

One of the joys of working in schools can be the opportunity to build relationships in an informal manner with children. These snapshot conversations that take place on the corridor and give us an insight into children's lives are so important for our relationship building. It can be very difficult to retain any of this information, let alone remember to ask about it again. However, if we are able to do this it can have a huge impact. As adults we know how it feels if someone remembers to ask us about something we have shared with them; we feel listened to, understood and validated for being important and worth thinking about and remembering. Imagine how powerful this would feel to a child, especially a child who is not used to this happening and imagine how good it may make them feel. For a child who is not used to adults outside of school showing them much interest, it can make them feel special and interesting if an adult in school asks them if the dog is better now or how their new baby brother is doing.

Reflect: Draw the path of your life

- On a large sheet of paper draw the path of your life from the age of five up to now.
- Include significant situations, events and people.
- Reflect on where and how the people influenced you.
- What did they say and do?
- How did they make you feel?
- Can you do that for a child at school now?

Provide positive messages to children

I am sure we can all remember significant people that have had an influence on our lives. They may have impacted on the way we think and view things or the choices we now make in our lives. When I was 10, I remember my class teacher taking me to the staff room with her when she had her preparation time as I was too disruptive to be left in the class without her. She used to draw lines in pencil to divide the lines in my book and I had to try and write underneath the bottom line to help me practise my handwriting, which was very untidy. I remember feeling very important, pleased that she wanted to help me and determined to improve my handwriting. My writing changed significantly for the better that year because of the time and commitment my teacher gave me and the messages she provided about wanting to help me.

Staff strategy – choose a child

Choose a child you feel would benefit from some extra adult input in their lives. Choose one thing you could do each day for a week to provide a positive message to them. You can use ideas from the list below or think of your own alternatives:

- Ask how their day is going.
- Ask them if they would like to help you do a job with their friend.
- Acknowledge something positive about them.
- Remember something about them and share it with them.
- Ask something about them.

Don't underestimate the crucial role you can play in changing a child's experience of life and relationships. It may not be noticeable immediately or measurable straight away but you never know what seeds you have planted or when they will grow. All school staff have a responsibility to invest time, thought, energy and commitment into exploring how they can contribute to and enhance children's emotional well-being on a daily basis. Every member of school staff has a role to play in helping children reach their full potential. You have to believe you can make a difference and start making it today.

Think of Jim

From 0–10 years Jim hears what a bad person he is at home every day. His behaviour at school is challenging and disruptive. The school staff find it hard to manage his behaviour and unconsciously reinforce the messages he has received at home that he is a bad person.

From 10–20 years Jim struggles with friendships and relationships and is often in trouble with the police.

From 20–30 years Jim criticises and struggles to manage his own children's behaviour and have a good relationship with them.

From 30–40 years Jim's kids don't want to see him and he is drinking heavily to drown out the internal voice that keeps telling him he's a bad person.

- Imagine if at aged 5 Jim had been a pupil at your school.
- Imagine if he had been flooded with messages that told him he was a good person.
- Imagine if he had experienced the school staff as showing him he was a worthwhile person who had good qualities to share with the world.
- Imagine if he had taken that confidence and self-esteem and positive sense of himself with him when he left the school.
- Imagine what his life could have been like at age 20, 30 or 40.
- Imagine if he had been lucky enough to come to your school.

Making schools happier places

Reflect: Stop for a minute

Ask yourself the following questions:

- Why did I want to work in a school?
- What did I want to achieve?
- Have I achieved this?
- What can I do tomorrow to make the school a happier place for the children?

In order to make a school a happier place for the children, parents and staff who use them, every member of school staff could contribute one small thing every day. This can contribute to changing the atmosphere and ethos of the school and is achievable by everyone showing a commitment. The quality of the relationships between children, parents and staff can change by smiling as you walk around the school. I work in several different schools during the week and certainly do not know the names of all the children and parents, but I smile at them as I walk around the school. I acknowledge children if they hold open a door for me (which they do frequently) by saying 'Thanks for holding the door open for me, that's very kind of you', or 'That's thoughtful of you.' This enables the child to know that I not only appreciate them holding the door, but I also experience them as being kind or thoughtful. How often do we see children showing us kind, caring, thoughtful behaviour in school but choose not to acknowledge it or are too busy to do so? Let's commit to changing this and providing children with positive feelings about who they are and what they do as often as we can during each school day. If we believe in children, we enable them to believe in themselves.

Every child has the right to be happy, settled and achieving their full potential in school; is this true for every child in your school? If not, is there anything you can do to make a difference?

Part Two: Practice

Using group work to promote emotional health and well-being and manage children's behaviour

7 The benefits of group work

The second section of this book explores the group work programmes that involve a focused approach to help children to deal with many of the issues discussed in the first section of the book. The group work sessions provide a safe and structured environment, which enables children to practise and develop new skills. The friendship group supports children who require additional support in developing and sustaining friendships, managing relationships, and dealing with conflict. The self-esteem group supports children who require additional support to develop confidence and self-esteem. Children can develop both sets of skills from participating in either programme, and they also contribute to the development and resilience. The group work programme in this book is carefully structured and the activities are clear, simple and easy to follow because the focus is on the relationships within the group and enabling children to make changes in their behaviour.

The rules for the group are negotiated and agreed with the children at the start of the first week and are revisited at the start of every session. This is discussed in more detail in Chapter Eight. The children are encouraged to decide the rules and contribute the ideas themselves, providing an opportunity for them to be listened to and valued for their opinion as well as being able to learn about choices, consequences and personal responsibility. The rules can be added to each week as the children become more confident in sharing ideas and contributing to the group. The group facilitator can ensure that certain rules are introduced each week if they will support the development of new skills for the children; for example, introducing the idea of being patient if the children are finding this difficult to do. The exploratory manner used by the facilitator to introduce this idea enables a discussion to take place about the meaning of the word and how the group can use it. This child-focused approach may result in a clearer understanding and more willing implementation from the children.

Opportunity to change behaviour

The experience of being part of a small group in a safe and supportive environment provides children with the opportunity to experiment with alternative ways of behaving if they wish to. The group facilitator encourages this process by offering praise and encouragement, along with acknowledging how difficult it can be to make changes.

Case study

Max, aged 5, was very quiet in the group. He found it difficult to share his ideas and spoke in a very soft voice so it was hard to hear and understand him. The other children sometimes spoke for him and appeared to find it hard to wait for him to get his words out.

Possible reasons for Max's behaviour:

- There was a history of drug and alcohol abuse in his family.
- He had recently been taken into foster care and had become even more quiet and withdrawn.

The teaching assistant who was facilitating the group commented on Max's struggle and acknowledged this by reflecting, 'Sometimes it can be really hard to speak, but remember in here you can share your ideas if you want to, and if you don't want to that's ok. We can all help you with this.' This reflection acknowledged the difficulty he was having and encouraged him to try and practise within the group. This enabled Max to use the experience of being in the group as an opportunity to practise changing behaviour that he found difficult. On the last week the activity involved making a medal, Max stood up along with the other children and was able to show his medal to the group. The teaching assistant acknowledged this big and positive change in Max by acknowledging how brave he had been.

The support and acceptance provided by the other children in the group and the facilitator enabled Max to experiment with a new behaviour in a safe environment. The facilitator was able to see and acknowledge his progress each week and comment 'You are doing so well at speaking in the group Max, I know that's a really hard thing to do.' This encouraged Max to persevere and make changes to his behaviour.

The experience of being in the small group enabled him to practise and become competent at adjusting to an expectation of school and society in general, i.e. speaking to others. The predictable format of the sessions provided him with a sense of stability, which enabled him to feel safe to experiment making changes within the group. The facilitator's encouragement and understanding of Max's behaviour helped to connect rather than separate them as they worked alongside each other to facilitate this change. This heightened self-confidence within the group setting increased as the sessions progressed and became noticeable to his class teacher and foster carer outside of the group.

The following examples are taken from children in schools who have experienced the group work programme:

Table 7.1 Impact of group work programme

Behaviour before the group	Behaviour after the group
Needing frequent adult approval	More confident and less demanding of adult attention
Unwilling to try and do things themselves	Happy to try and do things for themselves
Not contributing ideas to class discussions	Happy to share their thoughts and ideas
Shouting out all the time	Able to wait their turn and be patient
Not wanting to show their work	Being proud to share their work
Being quiet and reserved	Speaking out and being more confident
Frequently saying they feel unwell	No longer saying they feel unwell unless they are
Interrupting frequently	Able to wait their turn
Easily distracted and poor concentration	Improved concentration and attention span
Telling tales and lying about other children	More popular, no longer telling lies
Restless and fidgety	More settled and focused
Regular tantrums and angry outbursts	Calmer and happier in themselves

Belonging and ownership

The rules of the group are clear and devised with input from the children, enabling them to feel a sense of ownership and inclusion as they develop the social skills necessary for the group to function effectively. This sense of belonging and experience of having their voice heard is particularly important for children who may not have this experience at home or may feel marginalised in the rest of their school life. Some children may encounter feelings of loneliness, isolation and rejection both at home and school and the chance to be part of something on a weekly basis may help with this. This sense of belonging and feeling that they have something of value to contribute may enable them to develop positive feelings about themselves, resulting in increased confidence and self-esteem.

Children want and need:

● to be accepted;
● to be valued;
● to feel they have something to offer;
● to feel good about themselves.

Consistency

The group is held at the same time on the same day and in the same place each week; for example, Monday 10–10.35 am in the resource room. This consistency and predictability can reduce anxiety levels for the children and help them to feel safer in school. The sessions are clearly structured with a beginning, middle and end activity each week. The focus on time and acknowledging to the children when they have five minutes left, if they are involved in making something, provides a sense of reliability as they know what will happen, rather than finishing abruptly, which can increase anxiety. The sessions start and end in a similar way each week with the main activity changing, enabling the children to adjust to being back in the group by providing them with something familiar. This structure and regularity is crucial to the group work programme and the sense of belonging that is developed by the children. It provides an opportunity to be able to respond to organisation and predictable routines, which some of the children may not have much experience of. This also helps them to feel secure and more settled in school, often resulting in them being able to manage the time outside of the group more effectively.

The activities and sessions are planned and organised in a way that enables the children to practise new skills such as negotiating, planning and predicting. They discuss topics such as feeling proud, individuality and difference, validating and affirming the feelings that may be evoked by these. Children can experience the peer reactions to the situations that occur in the group as a way of normalising their behaviour, with reflections and commentary from the facilitator. 'Joe looked a bit cross that Sunita went first, but remember that we all have a turn to go first in this group and it will be your turn next week Joe.' The development of self-control is a process that lasts a lifetime and the more opportunities that children have to develop self-awareness with the support of a nurturing adult, the increased likelihood of them developing the skills for themselves. All these skills are crucial factors in the development of resilience.

Choices and consequences

The sessions provide children with the opportunity to understand about choices and consequences and the impact of these on the others in the group, as well as themselves. They are encouraged to think about and share how they feel about positive comments made to themselves by the other members of the group and the facilitator is encouraged to address negative comments or criticisms in an open and honest way.

For example, when carrying out the activity decorating a butterfly together (week two friendship programme) Taylor, aged 6, said 'That's not good colouring Ben. Do it neatly.' The facilitator reflected by saying 'It can feel really difficult when we are making something together and we are not happy with it or feel we would have liked it to be done differently.' She then explored with the whole group how that comment may have made Ben feel and encouraged him to say how it felt hearing it. This was carried out in a sensitive way without shaming Taylor and was used as an opportunity to increase the group's awareness of how the words we use may impact on other people. This enabled the children to gain an insight into their own feelings as well as those of others, resulting in them developing a more extensive emotional vocabulary and an increased sensitivity towards each other. The development of understanding and compassion for others is a crucial part of children learning self-acceptance and self-compassion. The opportunity to experience this within an emotionally safe and nurturing small group environment increases their understanding and the likelihood of them implementing it outside of the group setting.

Developing new skills

The activities enable the children to gain a sense of achievement and the focus is on the effort made and the process, rather than the end product. They are designed to help the children experience success and gain mastery through challenge and perseverance. This is supported by focused help from the group facilitator if needed. This development of new skills may be transferred outside of the group where other tasks may be greeted with effort and determination, rather than helplessness and resignation to failure. The tasks are planned to promote the skills we want the children to develop; for example, making a kind words balloon that consists of each child choosing a word to describe the other children in the group. This involves them thinking about other people and identifying and sharing their strengths with them (week six self-esteem group). The activities provide an opportunity for the facilitator to explore the skills the children think may be useful for them to use when they are working on the task along with introducing new vocabulary and discussing these concepts with them. For example, checking if they understand what working together and being patient mean, how these skills can be used and what potential difficulties may arise from this.

As part of the friendship programme the children are encouraged to practise the skills they have worked on in the session outside of the group during the week. These skills are discussed in the session and involve them practising friendship skills and are then discussed at the start of the following session. The feelings evoked by these situations are openly acknowledged and reflected upon. This enables the children to implement their new skills and see the immediate results of this behaviour for themselves along with building their confidence and self-esteem. This is discussed more fully in Chapter Eleven.

Validating feelings

An important role of the facilitator is to validate feelings and through the activities acknowledge that all feelings are acceptable. For example, week five of the friendship group involves an activity with different scenarios and the feelings they may evoke, such as sadness. The activity enables the children to understand their own feelings and those of other people and to integrate them more easily. The sessions are focused on sharing how things feel and the safe environment created by the facilitator enables children to discuss feelings in a more relaxed way and gradually share their own as they become more confident. However, while the sessions encourage the children to share their own thoughts and feelings, they are also given permission not to do this if they feel uncomfortable. This is crucial in ensuring that children feel safe and comfortable within the sessions and are able to choose when and how they contribute.

The friendship programme involves an activity in week three where each child makes a bookmark for another child in the group. This provides an ideal opportunity to explore how it feels to make something for someone else and what feelings it may activate. It enables a further discussion of other times when they may be able to do things for other people and the potential benefits of this. They are encouraged to thank each other for making the bookmark and then share how it feels when someone thanks you for something you have done for them. This enables the development of new skills both personally and socially, as well as the opportunity to experience sharing feelings in a positive and welcoming environment. They are also developing a sense of personal responsibility as a result of being part of a group, but making individual choices about what they share and how they behave within the group. This can result in an increased awareness of themselves and how their behaviour and choices impact on other people. This may manifest itself in a positive way outside of the group and the children may develop an increased awareness of themselves, resulting in a heightened awareness of other people. A member of school staff commented on this increased self-awareness in the children and said 'I know the children who have experienced the group work programmes because they start holding the doors open for other people around school.'

Building relationships

The experience of delivering group work provides the facilitator with the opportunity to focus on and get to know the children in a more relaxed way. It enables them to build a connection and get to know them better. This can help the other adults in school to build a relationship with the children as they are able to share relevant strategies of how to do this. The building of strong relationships with children gives powerful messages to them that school staff will support them and help them with their behaviour if they need it.

Case study

Ellie, aged 7, found it very difficult to sit on her chair during the group sessions and would often rock, sway from side to side and lie with her head on the table.

Possible reasons for Ellie's behaviour:

- Ellie was very anxious as her dad had left home a month ago and she hadn't seen him since.
- Mum had recently had a new baby who was sharing Ellie's room with her and waking up several times during the night.

The learning mentor who facilitated a self-esteem group with Ellie was able to support her by acknowledging 'It can be really hard to sit still on those chairs, I wonder if it would help if I pushed it in a bit for you?' This gentle and nurturing response enabled Ellie to manage to sit still for slightly longer and the learning mentor praised her for this by reflecting 'I can see you are trying really hard to sit still on your chair, well done.' This positive response motivated Ellie to keep trying to sit still and she was able to manage this for a bit longer each week. The learning mentor shared with her class teacher the strategies she had used to develop a relationship with her and encouraged her to try implementing the techniques in class with Ellie on a daily basis. These included ensuring that he explained where he was going when he was out of the class and when he would be returning. He also focused on acknowledging and praising the small amounts of time that Ellie was able to sit still, which resulted in her feeling less anxious and more relaxed in class.

The group work opportunity also provides a chance for children who struggle with and/or actively avoid adult relationships to have a more intimate experience of this. This can feel safer and less intense as other children are present and the relationship can be developed gradually in a more diluted way. It enables staff to relate to the children in a more relaxed way, to enjoy their personality and get to know and acknowledge their qualities, as well as offering a high level of support and attention.

The learning mentor who had delivered a group with Ellie noticed that she smiled at her on the corridor around school after the group had finished. The caring and nurturing response to helping her to practise changing a behaviour she had previously found difficult increased her confidence and self-esteem, resulting in her developing and maintaining a new relationship with a member of staff around school. It can sometimes be easy for children like Ellie to go unnoticed in class as they may not present challenging behaviour or disrupt the class. However, these children need help just as much as the children who are showing confrontational behaviour, often more so as they may be more easily overlooked.

Staff development

The school staff who deliver the groups are able to gain awareness of how they relate to the pupils and learn new skills to improve their relationships. They also increase their perception of how they communicate with children, along with a deeper understanding of children's emotional and social developmentl e.g. Kathy was a very skilled teaching assistant who was good at building relationships with the children. However, she admitted that she sometimes struggled with developing and maintaining boundaries with the children, especially around finishing time if they were enjoying doing something. Her activities in class often ran over and she acknowledged that her time management was poor.

The experience of delivering the group work enabled her to practise new ways of working and to practise working to the times allocated for the activities. The five minute warning she gave to the group before they finished the main activity allowed her to see that the children were happy with this as long as they knew what was happening and why. It enabled her to gain a better understanding of some of the emotional reactions and behaviour she had experienced from children in the past when she had expected them to just stop what they were doing. She transferred this time warning to the activities she carried out in class and was pleased to experience the results from the children being the same, along with helping her to improve an aspect of her work.

Delivering the group work programme provides the facilitator with an ideal opportunity to develop new skills that can be transferred to their role outside of the group. The heightened awareness of children's emotional needs and the use of reflective language can both be integrated into the facilitator's existing role in school in a way that promotes their confidence and enhances their contribution to the rest of the staff team.

Positive messages

The use of reflective language throughout the group work sessions provides the children with a very positive message about themselves as it communicates 'I can see you, I am trying to understand you, whatever you are thinking or feeling is ok, you are worth thinking about and I am interested in getting to know you.' All these responses reinforce that the child is important as an individual in their own right and provides a clear sense of acceptance of who they are as a person. The programme promotes an awareness of the children's own emotions along with sensitivity to the emotions of other people, resulting in an increased ability to put those feelings into words. The experience of the group work programmes and the facilitators' reflections given to the children are positive and powerful and for some children may provide new opportunities for them to be experienced in this way. The facilitator's use of reflective language enables the children to feel seen, heard, valued and understood – all essential ingredients to build their confidence and self-esteem.

Figure 7.1 Positive messages to children

Communication skills

The group work provides an opportunity to develop children's social and communication skills and enables some children to find their voice for the first time, while others can practise being less domineering towards other people. For example, Mohammed, aged 7, was referred to the group by his class teacher who found him very difficult to have in class as he was constantly talking, interrupting and calling out. This was impacting on his learning and friendships as the other children in the class were irritated by his behaviour. Mohammed showed this behaviour through the first group work session, but with reflections such as 'I can see you really want to say something Mohammed but I'd like you to try and practise waiting quietly while I listen to Chloe, and then we can listen to you.' Or 'Well done for being patient, I know that's difficult.'

Mohammed was gradually able to wait for longer and by the fourth session was able to listen more to the other children in the group. As he knew she would have his turn eventually, this lessened his anxiety and enabled her to practise patience and self-regulation. I spoke to his class teacher and encouraged her to try this reflection with him in class and she was pleased with the results and found he was calling out far less than he had been before the group. This increased self-knowledge and self-awareness resulted in a change in his behaviour and an increase in popularity with his peers in class.

New opportunities

There are children in our schools who have learnt to hide themselves and their needs and instead have developed a way of being that puts everyone else's needs before their own. These children are often invisible in schools as their behaviour may not outwardly present as a concern, especially if there are a number of children who show their feelings in a more challenging way. The group work programmes provide an ideal opportunity for these otherwise invisible children to become more visible within the sessions and to start understanding and expressing their needs and wishes. There have been several examples of these children actively showing more confidence and having more of a presence in school. One teacher told me, 'He even walks differently now, I hadn't realised how much he was stooping until he started holding his head up high.'

The early messages some children receive about not being seen or heard may result in them finding it difficult to speak out in any situation and being quiet and withdrawn in an attempt not to draw attention to themselves. For these children the group work programmes provide an ideal opportunity for them to practise finding their voice and sharing their thoughts and feelings within a smaller group, if they wish to. As these children develop more confidence in speaking in front of their peers, these skills may then become transferable to the larger group within the classroom. The permissive and accepting environment created by the facilitator within the group sessions can enable children to feel noticed in a less threatening and exposing way than in a whole class situation. The reflective language used by the facilitator can enable the child to feel more confident at speaking out.

For example, Sam, aged 7, was very quiet in class and his teacher described him as a child that was always eager to please. She described an experience of him bringing in some sweets for his birthday and giving them out to the other children in his class and not having any for himself. This made me wonder what early messages Sam had received which had resulted in him believing that his needs didn't matter. In the group work sessions he was very quiet and waited until the other children had chosen the felt pen they wanted to use before choosing his. I encouraged the facilitator to offer the pens round the group the following week, starting with Sam, and to acknowledge 'It's really important that we all have a chance to choose which colour pen we want to use.' The facilitator used this kind of reflection each week during the activities and gently encouraged Sam to find his voice by reflecting, 'Sometimes we can think other people's ideas are better than ours and that can make us not want to speak, but in here everyone's ideas are important.'

This experience may also benefit children who find it hard to make decisions for themselves. When adults are always in control and making choices for children, it is not surprising that children may present as helpless and unable to do this. The opportunities created by the group work experience enable children to make choices and decisions by the activities that are included, along with encouraging each child to have a voice and share their thoughts and ideas. For example, making a poster about something I like (week two self-esteem group), enables children to choose what they would like to include and how they want to share it with the rest of the group. If a child finds this hard they are provided with additional reassurance and acknowledgement of their feelings by the group facilitator.

The group work experience introduces many new ideas and concepts to the children. Along with the development of social and emotional skills, it can also expand the children's vocabulary by introducing new words in the context of the sessions; for example, exploring with children words such as 'patient' and 'lonely' and ensuring they know what they mean. After several sessions with a child who kept interrupting, another child in the group said 'Well done for being patient Mario' to him. He had understood the word patient and was able to use it in an appropriate context after hearing me using it and explaining its meaning for several weeks.

Affirmative responses

Throughout the facilitator's guidelines I suggest reflecting 'You may need some help from an adult with this, and I can help you if you would like me to.' This reflection provides the message that sometimes children need help from an adult and it is acceptable to ask for it. This is particularly important for children who have learnt self-sufficiency at a young age and will struggle on their own as they have learnt 'It's not ok to ask for help or even if you do no one helps you.' It enables the child to have the choice and decide if they need help, rather than the adult controlling the situation and deciding for them. I encourage the facilitator to say 'help from an adult' as a generic term rather than 'help from me' as this reinforces that other adults outside of the group may also be able to help if they need it and gives the message that it's acceptable to ask them.

Positive changes in children

The benefits to the children of being in the group work sessions can become apparent to the facilitators as the sessions progress. They may see changes such as increased confidence, more willing to speak out, being able to be patient while others speak. The class teachers have commented on improved concentration, improved peer relationships, more able to recognise, express and manage their feelings and more empathy with others. Some children have identified and shared the benefits themselves such as 'I like being in this group', 'I've got more friends', and 'I'm doing better at my work'. Some parents have also noticed the differences in their children since being in the group work sessions and have said 'He's much happier in himself now', 'He's getting on much better with his brother' and 'She's much calmer and can tell me if she's upset now.' These are examples of the visible impact but there may be many more that are less visible and that may only be noticed in specific situations; for example, less anxious about tests and more able to cope with losing.

The overall experience of being part of the group can not only be beneficial for school staff and individual children, but it can also highlight areas of concern and need for children that may otherwise be unnoticed. This provides the school with the opportunity to respond to this in a way that ensures they are meeting each child's emotional and social needs and promoting a whole school approach to children's mental health and well-being.

8   The role of the group facilitator

The group facilitator can be a learning mentor, teaching assistant, support worker, family worker or other role within the school who has a thorough understanding of children's social and emotional development and is confident at working with small groups. They need to be interested in emotional well-being and developing new skills to manage children's behaviour, have a capacity for some self-reflection, and a willingness to try using the reflective language skills described.

The groups are most effective when they are implemented following the clear time guidelines set out in the group work packs as this enables the sessions to be structured and organised. The format is deliberately prescriptive and enables the facilitator to be exploratory with the children. There is a resource list for each six-week programme and these must be ready at the start of each session before the children come in. It is useful to allocate an hour to the facilitator for each group to allow for time to set out resources and clear away, reflect on the session and write brief session notes at the end of the group. They will also need some time to be allocated at the end of each six-week group to write a brief report on each child. This is discussed in more detail later in the chapter.

Completing questionnaires for the group

In order to maximise the benefits of the group work experience for the children, it is useful to complete a questionnaire for each child at the start and end of the intervention (see resources section). This enables any changes that children have made to be monitored, along with identifying children who may benefit additional support. The questionnaires are in the resources section and can be photocopied for each child. They can be completed by the child's teacher or by a teaching assistant who knows the child well. It is important that the start and end questionnaires are completed by the same person wherever possible. There is more information on how to complete the questionnaires in the group work questionnaire guidelines sheet in the resources section.

Developing new relationships

The group work sessions provide the facilitator with an ideal opportunity to develop their relationship with the identified children and practise a new way of managing their behaviour by acknowledging and reflecting their feelings. For example, providing gentle reminders of the rules and acknowledging that it can be hard to remember new rules can be an effective way of supporting rather than penalising children. For example, Cara, aged 6, was absent on the second session and at the start of the third week kept calling out when other children were talking. I acknowledged that it was particularly hard for her to remember the rules as she had missed the session last week and wondered if the other children had any ideas for how they could help her with this. The rest of the group suggested going through the rules again to help them all remember, which was an effective way of supporting them all and helping Cara too.

At the start of each session after setting out the folders and resources and ensuring the group rules are visible to each child, the children are collected from their class and brought to the room. This is an important part of the process and gives a message of caring and nurture to the children. The children can be excited, scared and anxious at the start of the sessions, particularly the first one when they are unsure what will be happening. It can be useful to acknowledge this to them, e.g. 'It may feel a bit strange coming out of class with me, but I will explain what we will be doing when we get to the room.' This can help to reduce any feelings of anxiety and fear. The use of reflections provides all the following positive messages to the children and can be a useful way to identify the impact of its use.

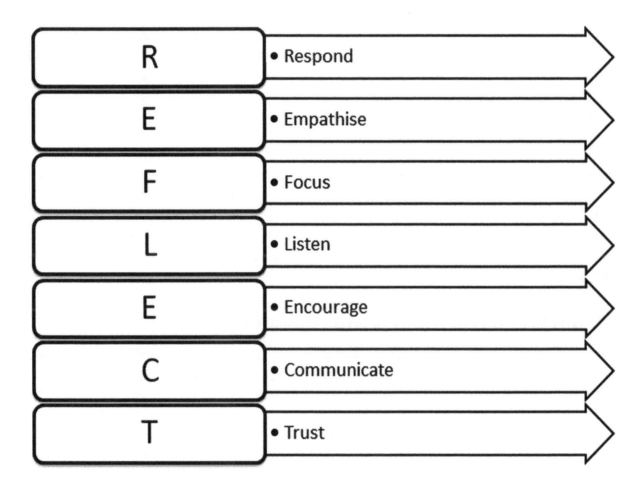

Figure 8.1 Positive impact of reflecting

Sharing information with other people

There may be opportunities to share relevant information with children's parents or carers if this is appropriate. For example, if a child is trying hard to change their behaviour or has made a positive contribution to the group it may be useful to share this with their parent. This information can be shared in order to highlight the effort the child is making and to enable the parent or carer to support this behaviour at home. The friendship programme includes tasks that can be implemented outside of the group on a weekly basis and it may be helpful to share this with the parent or carer to provide a clearer understanding of the group and to give them the opportunity to support this process if they are willing.

It can also be useful to share relevant information with the children's class teacher on a weekly basis so they can follow the child's process. For example, sharing that a quiet child has spoken for the first time and how this occurred. If children appear to be responding to particular reflections it is useful to share these with the class teacher who may also choose to use a similar response to help a child. Other school staff, including lunchtime organisers, teaching assistants and the head teacher, may also benefit from receiving feedback on the changes a child is working on within the group, so they are able to support this and acknowledge it to the child if appropriate.

Identifying children who may benefit from further support

The group work programme may identify children who need further intervention or specific focused help with particular areas. The facilitator will need to share this information with a more senior member of staff within the school such as the SENCO (special educational needs coordinator) in order to build on the work of the group where necessary. This can also be highlighted on the group work report under the section on recommendations. It is also essential that any concerns, a child disclosing or child protection concerns, are recorded and passed on to the relevant member of staff, in line with the school's child protection procedure.

Writing reports

At the end of the six-week group it is useful for the group facilitator to complete a report for each child. The format and a completed example of this are included in the resources section. The report provides a short summary of the child's experiences of being in the group and identifies any recommendations that may assist the child further. This may include support from within school or on occasion help from outside agencies such as a mental health team. The report should include any additional comments from school staff as the example demonstrates. A copy of the report can be given to the allocated person in your school, e.g. SENCO, head teacher, etc. along with the child's start and end of intervention questionnaires.

9 Starting and ending group work

The groups work well with a maximum of four children all from the same year group and preferably the same class to ensure the maximum impact of transferable skills on their return to class. They can also be delivered with a pair of children to provide a more intense and focused intervention, which can be useful for children who need extra support with sharing, waiting their turn and other social and emotional skills. This enables them to achieve success within a more realistic environment, which can then encourage them to practise these skills outside of the group on a weekly basis.

Group composition

The group should consist of either all the same gender or an equal mix of girls and boys. It is also useful to consider the developmental levels of the children that are to be in the same group to ensure that they will be able to manage the tasks at a similar pace and level. The personalities of the children can be considered too so there are combinations of dominant and less dominant children who can all be provided with support to make changes with their behaviour. Children can participate in both of the group work programmes, but this would be most effective if there was a period of time in between to integrate the skills they have learnt.

When considering the group composition it is essential to consider each child's individual needs to ensure the group's success and the children's emotional safety. It is aimed at children who are low-level disrupters and children who would benefit from additional focused support, rather than children who have more complex needs and may require more specialised intervention. If a child presents with very challenging behaviour and has complex needs then being in a group may be too intense and overwhelming, resulting in the child sabotaging the group as a way of managing their feelings. For these children, the activities can be delivered with one other child who has been identified as a role model, so the facilitator is able to provide more focused support. This may enable them to practise different ways of behaving and have this modelled for them in a nurturing environment.

Children who may benefit from the group work programme include:

- Children who lack confidence or have low self-esteem.
- Children who find it hard to make and keep friends.
- Children who are quiet and withdrawn.
- Children who are pleasers and feel their own needs are not important.
- Children who interrupt and find it hard to listen.
- Children who find it hard to share and take turns.
- Children who tell lies.
- Children who find it hard to make mistakes.
- Children who have regular conflict with other children.

- Children who bully others or who are bullied themselves.
- Children who are restless and find it hard to concentrate.
- Children who are anxious, worried or fearful.
- Children who lack resilience.
- Children who lack self-awareness.
- Children who are experiencing changes at home such as a new baby, etc.

The group is an ideal opportunity to boost children who are not as happy or settled as they could be or achieving their full potential.

Format of the sessions

The sessions are held for thirty-five minutes once a week for six weeks. As mentioned in previous chapters, it is an essential part of the process that it is held at the same time, same day and in the same room each week as this models consistency, predictability and provides structure to their week. The room must be available each week and have a table and chairs for everyone. Ideally this can be a small room where there may be minimal external distractions to enable the children to focus on the group. It is *essential* that the group is not disturbed by other people who need resources from the room or wish to use it as this can be very disruptive and gives a message that the group is not important. A sign on the door at the start of the session (see resources section) and a reminder at staff meetings can ensure there are no interruptions.

The room needs to convey a positive and welcoming message to the children as they enter it. The physical and emotional environment that is being provided by the group work is crucial to its success and impact. For some children whose lives outside of school may be chaotic and unpredictable, the calm, tidy and peaceful environment will enable them to feel safe and to settle more easily. They may be more aware of their physical and emotional environment and therefore the group work setting can provide an opportunity to relax and enjoy their time in the group.

Starting something new can make some children feel very anxious and scared. It is important that this is acknowledged (see facilitator's guidelines for week one for reflections to use). If a child looks anxious or uncertain it may be due to hyper vigilance and it is crucial that this is acknowledged. If the facilitator reflects on this and notices what the child is doing, e.g. 'I can see you looking at all the collage materials, maybe you're wondering what we are going to do in here today, I'll tell you when everyone has sat down'. This provides a strong message of acknowledgement and validation to the child along with reassuring them.

When the children have all sat down in their spaces chosen by the facilitator, explain to them that this is a group that will meet every week in the same room for six weeks for thirty-five minutes and show them the start and end times on the clock. Explain it will meet at the same time and the same day each week and that if you are absent then they will not lose that session – it will be carried out the following week when you are back in school. Explain that the group will start and end in the same way each week and there will be a different activity in the middle. Discuss that the group is a way of helping them to practise and develop new skills such as sharing and taking turns and the activities will provide ways to help them with this. The facilitator's guidelines (see Chapters Eleven and Twelve) provide detailed step-by-step information for each session and it is useful to read these in advance of the sessions to ensure they are understood and can be followed easily. They provide clear explanations for the beginning, middle and end of each session, along with suggested reflections that may be useful to use with the children.

On the first week each child is provided with a sticker with their name on it to wear for the session. This is to help the facilitator to get to know everyone and for the children to get to know each other if they are not in the same class. This is not necessary if the facilitator already knows the children and they are in the same class. During the main activity the children will sometimes be working in pairs. It is important that the children all have the opportunity to work with different people during these tasks as this will help them to develop new friendships and skills.

The facilitator must ensure they follow the time guidelines set out in the group work pack as this will enable the group to run smoothly. At the end of the session acknowledge their hard work, tell them you will see them next week and walk them back to their class. The facilitator needs some time at the end of each session to complete the register and session detail sheet (see resources section). The session detail sheet will provide a brief overview of how the facilitator feels the session went and a few sentences on each child, e.g. 'The children all enjoyed making the bookmarks for each other and were much better at following the group rules this week. Marcus worked well with Tai and was very patient while they were colouring the butterfly together. He seems to be more confident than he was and is contributing his ideas more.'

Each child will be given a folder of the same colour for them to keep the activities in. They will also have a session chart to colour, which shows how many sessions they are having and provides a structured beginning to each week as they colour in the appropriate number chart (see resources section). If a child is absent then they colour in the session number they have missed on their return so everyone's chart is the same.

They keep the session chart in their folder and these are set out for them on the table when they come to each session and can be in the same place each week depending on the format of the activity and the needs of the children. The group facilitator keeps the folders and their contents in a safe place until the last session when the children can take them home if they want to. As this is explained to the group at the start of the first session, most children are ok with this. If a child finds this difficult it may tell us something about their experience of trust and can be reflected to them, e.g. 'It seems that you're really not sure about me looking after your folder, maybe it's hard for you to leave it with me, but that's one of our rules and I will keep it safe for you.'

Each session starts and ends in a similar way each week with an activity in the middle. It is useful to show the children on the clock how long they will spend with you so they are aware of this and it helps them manage the time. They will become familiar with the structure of the sessions very quickly and the predictability provides them with a sense of security. At the start of the first session after they have coloured in their session chart and the facilitator has explained about the folders, encourage the group to think of some group rules they will follow. The facilitator will explain to them that they need to think of ways to make sure that everyone enjoys being in the group and can start them off by giving them an example such as 'Listen when other people are talking.' The group can add to the rules each week if they need to, but they only need a few to ensure the group runs smoothly.

The rules are written out by the facilitator on a large card and put on the wall where everyone can see them. They are displayed for each session and can be referred to as a way of managing behaviour within the group. For example, 'I can see you really want to go first Jane, but remember one of our rules is that we take turns. When Joe has had his turn then it will be your go. I know it can feel hard but let's see if you are able to wait.' The facilitator may want to think of some rules beforehand if they think the children may struggle to identify their own or if there are children in the group who may need specific support, such as sharing the equipment for example.

Although it is beneficial if all the children participate in all the activities and contribute to the discussions, it is important that children are given the option not to share their thoughts and feelings if they do not feel comfortable. This needs to be explained to the children at the start of the group work sessions (see week one facilitator's guidelines for more detail). Once the sessions have progressed and the children are familiar with the format and feel relaxed, they are usually happy to contribute, but having the choice not to can help them with this. This is a crucial aspect of responding to children's individual needs and ensuring we focus on helping them to feel safe and secure before we expect them to change their behaviour. For example, a child who has been referred to the group because they find it hard to speak in class needs additional support along with feeling safe to develop the ability to do this.

Preparing for the group

In previous chapters I have discussed the importance of school staff using self-reflection as a tool to explore and monitor their own feelings. This is of particular value to the group facilitator and can be implemented by checking how they are feeling at the start and end of the session. It is good practice to have time to prepare the resources beforehand in a relaxed way rather than rushing around looking for them at the last minute. I encourage the facilitator to spend a few minutes sat in the room when it is prepared, before going to collect the children. Schools are extremely busy places and I appreciate how difficult this may be, but it is worth doing in order that the group is delivered in the most effective way possible. I suggest looking through the facilitator's guidelines and having them and the session plan accessible so they can be referred to easily. The children are usually too involved in the activities to look at them but the facilitator can acknowledge this by saying 'These notes are to help me run our group well and I want to look at them to make sure I do it properly so we all have an enjoyable time.' If a facilitator forgets something or makes a mistake then this should be acknowledged to the group. I once forgot to put their session charts out and I acknowledged it by saying I had forgotten and acknowledging that 'even adults forget things and make mistakes sometimes.' It is important that as adults we are able to model this for children as it gives permission for them to admit to their mistakes more easily.

The facilitator's use of their own internal check can be useful to develop self-awareness and appreciation of the importance of the tone of voice, body language and facial expressions being used. All of these will be communicating powerful messages to the children and are worth exploring and reflecting on afterwards. This can be useful to look at after the session when writing up the session notes, e.g. if a session was particularly challenging, first explore how you felt, were you hungry, tired and a bit distracted thinking about what you had to do after the session? As the group work is a focused programme with a small group of children, it can be intense and tiring. In order for it to run most effectively the facilitator should enjoy delivering the programme and look forward to its weekly occurrence, rather than dread it.

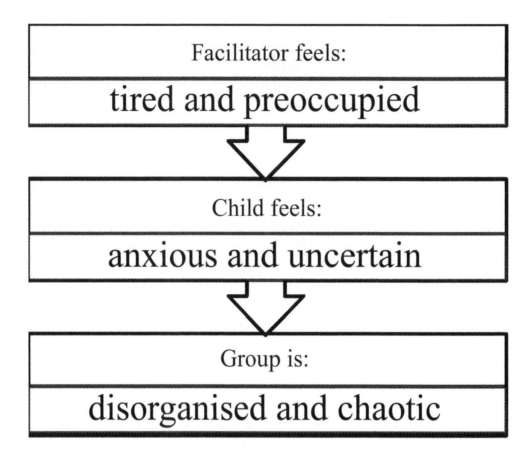

Figure 9.1 Potential negative impact of facilitator

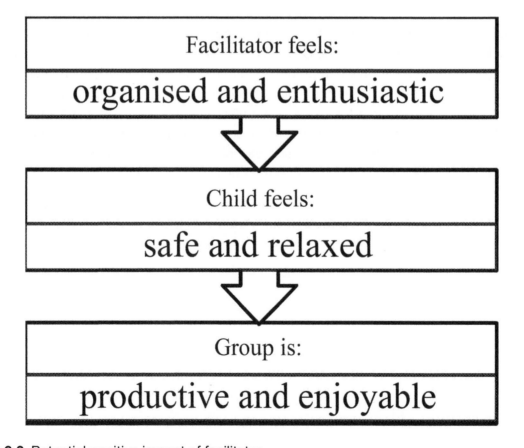

Figure 9.2 Potential positive impact of facilitator

The importance of endings

On the last session it is essential that the ending is acknowledged. For some children the group work opportunity has been the highlight of their week and it is important that the loss of the weekly sessions is given the appropriate validation. There may be children in the group who have experienced many changes and losses in their lives and these may not have been managed well, so it provides an opportunity for the group facilitator to provide them with a more positive experience. The ending of the group can be a good opportunity to validate the children's feelings about this and to be honest with them in a way that recognises and helps them manage their feelings.

The facilitator will start each session by stating the session number as the children are colouring in their session charts and acknowledge the remaining number of sessions. For example, 'It's our fourth session today so we have got two more sessions and then the sixth session will be our last one.' This provides the children with an opportunity to voice their feelings each week and provides the facilitator with insight into how each child manages endings. This information can be shared with the children's existing teacher to help them assist the child to manage changes that may occur in class and at the end of the school year. It can also be passed on to the child's new class teachers at the start of each year to enable them to manage the transition to their class in a way that meets the child's individual needs.

Case study

Broden, aged 7, stopped the group facilitator on the corridor regularly to check if she was collecting him on that day.

Possible reasons for this:

- Broden's dad had left when he was four and he hadn't seen or heard from him since.
- Broden's mum often promised that they would do things together and then forgot or changed her mind.

The group facilitator was able to provide him with reassurance, explain when she would be collecting him, acknowledge his feelings and ensure that she prepared him for the ending. She was also able to talk to his present class teacher to ensure that Broden was given advance warning of any changes wherever possible, and was always prepared for when his teacher was out of class and when she would be coming back.

The opportunity for children to participate in an ending in a positive way and have their feelings about this acknowledged and validated is essential for their emotional well-being. During the last session the facilitator is encouraged to express their feelings about the ending and acknowledge that this may be difficult for the children. They are encouraged to respond positively to the children's expression of their own feelings about the ending in a way that validates and 'contains' them. This positive event may provide the children with a completely different ending compared to others they have had previously where people may just disappear overnight with no explanation being offered to them. This experience of endings provides them with a new template that is crucial for their emotional health.

10 'What ifs' for group work

The following reactions to events are rare and may never happen, but it is useful to be prepared for any responses you may experience:

- If a child doesn't want to come to a session check with the child if there is a reason, reflect that 'It may feel a bit strange coming out of class' and encourage them to come: 'You can come and see what we are doing this week.' If they still choose not to come then say 'We'll miss you and I'll come and get you again next week.'
- If a child comes to the session but is reluctant to join in, reflect that 'Maybe you are unsure about joining in today, you can just watch and see what we are going to do and join in when you feel like it.'
- If a child is disrupting the session remind them of the ground rules and reflect that 'It can be hard following the rules but I'd really like you to . . .'
- If a child walks out of a session, remind them of the ground rules and encourage them to stay and reflect that 'Maybe you're unsure what we are going to do today; I wonder if it would help if you sat next to me?'
- If there are disruptions to the session by meetings taking place in the room or drums playing loudly nearby, ensure that all staff are made aware beforehand that the room will be used. If there is noise from outside then acknowledge this and reflect that 'It can be difficult to concentrate when there is a lot of noise outside.'
- If people walk in during the session, remind them you are doing the group and ask them to come back later, put a sign on the door (see resources section) and reflect that 'It's important that we're not disturbed because our time together is valuable.'
- If a child wants to take what they've made with them that week, reflect that 'You really want to take that with you today but you can take everything with you on the last week.'
- If a child shares something about themselves, e.g. 'I've not got a dad, I've just got a mum', listen to the child and respond appropriately; if the child needs to talk more, offer to have some time with them outside of the group where they can talk to you. Ensure you pass on any concerns to the relevant member of staff in school.
- If a child wants to give you their folder rather than take it with them, reflect that 'Maybe you want to leave me something to make sure I remember you, but I'll still see you around school and you can always come and talk to me if you'd like to.'
- If a child is absent on the last session, find the child when they are next in school, acknowledge that everyone missed them in the session and give them their folder.

11 Friendship programme and facilitator's guidelines

This chapter contains a weekly overview and facilitator's guidelines for each session. The weekly overview provides a summary of each week's session and activities. The facilitator's guidelines are more detailed and provide examples of reflections to use during the sessions. The group facilitator needs to take the facilitator's guidelines with them to each session.

The resources are in the resources section at the end of the book.

Overview: week one

Beginning (10 minutes)

- Introduce the group; explain about the time and number of sessions.
- Encourage each child to sit at the table, put their name sticker on (if applicable), colour their chart and write their name on their folder.
- Explain that you will look after their folder and that you will keep everything until the last session when they can take it with them if they want to.
- Explain that the group will start and end in the same way each week, but the activity in the middle will be different.
- Discuss the ground rules for the group, encourage them to contribute their ideas and write them up and display them.

Middle (20 minutes)

- Explain that this group is all about us making friends and that this week we will be talking about what is good about having friends, how they make us feel and what we like doing with our friends.
- Give each child a piece of paper and ask them to draw a picture of themselves playing with a friend.
- Explain that there is no right or wrong way of them doing this and they can choose who they draw and what they are doing.
- Ask them to share their pictures with the group and to explain to the rest of the group what they are doing and how it feels, e.g. 'We are playing football and I feel happy.'
- Encourage them to practise being a good friend this week and tell them that you will ask them about this next week.

Ending (5 minutes)

- Explain that each session will end in the same way each week.
- Ask them to share one thing they have learnt or enjoyed about being in the group today.
- Praise them for their hard work in the session today.

Facilitator's guide: week one

Beginning (10 minutes)

- If you already know the children and are not using the name stickers then indicate to the children where you would like them to sit.
- If you are using stickers put each child's name sticker out on the table, ensuring the children who will need the most support are sat next to you.
- Encourage them to find their sticker and sit at the table.
- Reflect that 'It may feel strange coming out of class with me today.'
- Reflect that 'It may feel uncomfortable at first as we don't know each other very well yet, but we will spend the next six weeks getting to know each other better.'
- Discuss that the group is a way of helping them to practise and develop new skills such as sharing, taking turns and being good friends, and that the activities will provide ways to help them with this.
- Explain that being in this group is a bit different to the rest of school because in here they can choose not to join in the discussions if they do not want to.
- Reflect that 'It's really important that you feel happy being in here and sharing your ideas, some children find this easy and other children find it difficult and that's because we are all different. It's ok in here if you need help with this and you can just say if you do not want to join in our discussions, but this group is to help make this easier for you to do.'
- If a child is looking around the room then reflect that 'I can see you are looking around the room, maybe it feels a bit strange coming in here.'
- Explain that you will see them every week for six weeks and if you need to miss a week due to a school trip or you being absent then they will have the session the following week so they will not miss the session.
- Tell them that you will see them at the same time on the same day each week and show them on the clock the start and end time.
- Give each child a folder and a session chart.
- Encourage them to colour in week one on their chart and say they can choose which colour to use.
- Ask them to put the chart in their folder when they have finished.
- If a child needs help with this reflect that 'It can be difficult to do this and I wonder if you would like some help with it?'
- Explain that they can write their name however they want to on their folder as it is theirs: 'You can do it in big or small writing wherever you want to as it's your folder.'
- If a child looks unsure reflect that 'It seems like you're not sure where or how to write it, but remember you can choose and there's no right or wrong way.'
- Collect the folders and explain that you will look after them until next week and say 'When you come in next week I will have your folder and colour chart set out waiting for you, just like I did this week. It may feel difficult leaving all your work in here but I will keep it safe for you and you can take everything with you on the last week.'
- Introduce them to the idea of ground rules for the group and encourage each child to contribute if they wish to; allow children to just observe and not contribute if they want to and reflect that 'It can be hard to think of things to say so don't worry if you can't think of a rule today, we will look at this again next week.'
- Write the ground rules for the group on card and display them so that all the children can see them easily.

- Explain that the rules will be up each week to help everyone to follow them.
- Acknowledge that 'It can be hard to remember the rules so this will help us to remember.'

Middle (20 minutes)

- Explain that this group is all about us making friends and that this week we will be talking about what is good about having friends, how they make us feel and what we like doing with our friends.
- Acknowledge that 'Making friends can be a difficult thing to do and in this group we will be practising lots of things that can help us with this.'
- Explain that they will be drawing a picture of themselves playing with a friend.
- Explain that this will be their picture and they can choose who they draw and what they are doing.
- Reflect that 'There is no right or wrong way of doing this because it's your picture.'
- If you notice a child looking at another child's picture or looking uncertain, reflect that 'It can be hard to decide what to do, I can see you looking at (other child's) picture and maybe you think you should do the same, but remember we are all different and our pictures will all be different too.'
- While they are drawing their pictures encourage them to think about things they like about their friends and qualities, such as they are kind, etc.
- Explore with them if they know what these words mean and discuss how they may use them, e.g. 'If someone falls over in the playground and you go and help them, then what qualities are you using?'
- Try and spend time focusing equally on each picture, but don't offer praise or positive comments yet as this may influence what the other children are doing on their picture.
- When they have completed their picture ask them to share them with the rest of the group and explain what they are doing and how it feels, e.g. 'We are playing football and I feel happy.'
- Acknowledge that 'It's not always easy to say how we feel, but in here we are going to be practising how to do this.'
- Reflect that 'Sometimes it can be really hard to speak, but remember in here you can share your ideas if you want to, and if you don't want to that's ok.'
- Praise them all for their hard work and thank them for sharing their pictures with the group.
- Encourage them to practise being a good friend this week outside of the group and remind them of the qualities you've talked about a good friend having, such as being kind, etc.
- Ask them to try and use these qualities this week and explain that you will ask them about this next week.
- Acknowledge that 'It can be hard to remember to do things so I will remind you if I see you around school.'

Ending (5 minutes)

- Explain that each session will end in the same way each week.
- Ask them to share one thing they have learnt or enjoyed about being in the group today.
- Praise them for their hard work in the session and tell them you will see them at the same time and in the same room next week.
- Walk them back to their class.

Overview: week two

Beginning (10 minutes)

- Encourage each child to colour their chart.
- Check if they remember the ground rules and ask if they want to add to them.
- Ask them to share examples of when they have been a good friend this week and how they felt when they were doing this.

Middle (20 minutes)

- Explain that this week we will be talking about working together and how this is something that a good friend can do.
- Ask them to share ideas of when they could work together and what they might do, talking about how it can feel.
- Give each pair a butterfly to colour and explain that they will do this together.
- Acknowledge that this may be difficult to do, but you will help them to work this out, e.g. 'It can be difficult when you both want to colour the same bit, I wonder how you can work that out?'
- Identify and discuss any difficulties as they arise, e.g. 'I can see you are trying to colour his eyes and it's hard for you to reach, I wonder what Sara could do to help you with that?'
- When they have finished, praise them and ask them to say what they liked or found difficult about it, e.g. sharing the paper.
- Explain that you will photocopy the butterfly for each pair so they have one each in their folder for next week.
- Encourage them to practise working together with other people on things this week and explain that you will ask them about this next week.

Ending (5 minutes)

- Explain that each session will end in the same way each week.
- Ask them to share one thing they have learnt or enjoyed about being in the group today.
- Praise them for their hard work in the session and tell them you will see them at the same time and in the same room next week.
- Walk them back to their class.

Facilitator's guide: week two

Beginning (10 minutes)

- Put each child's folder on the table in the same place as last week and put the ground rules up on the wall.
- Encourage them to find their folder and colour in their session chart.
- Acknowledge that you are pleased to see them all again.
- Encourage them to put their session chart in their folder.
- Show them the start and end time on the clock.

- Ask them if they can remember the ground rules and show them.
- Ask if anyone would like to add to the ground rules and remind them that it's ok if they don't want to.
- Ask them to share examples of when they have been a good friend this week and how they felt when they were doing it.

Middle (20 minutes)

- Explain that this week we will be talking about working together and how this is something that good friends can do.
- Acknowledge that 'There are lots of times when we need to work together so it's good to be able to practise this in our group.'
- Ask them to share ideas of when they have worked together and what they did, e.g. making something.
- Encourage them to talk about how it felt and prompt them if they find this difficult, e.g. 'It can feel fun to make something together.'
- If you notice a child is not contributing their ideas, reflect that 'It can be difficult to share our ideas sometimes, remember we can all do this if we want to.'
- Explain that they will be working in pairs and colouring a butterfly and give one to each pair.
- Acknowledge that this may be difficult to do, but you will help them to work this out, e.g. 'It can be difficult when you both want to colour the same bit, I wonder how you can work that out?'
- If they find this difficult, you can suggest ideas, e.g. 'I wonder if it might help if you colour the eyes while Jamie colours the body, sometimes we need help to work out how to do things.'
- While they are working together reflect that 'I can see you are both working together really well.'
- Identify and discuss any difficulties as they arise, e.g. 'I can see you are trying to colour his eyes and it's hard for you to reach, I wonder what Sara could do to help you with that?'
- While they are working on the butterfly encourage them to work together and ensure that all the children are contributing equally.
- When they have finished, praise them and ask them to say what they liked or found difficult about it, e.g. sharing the paper.
- Acknowledge any positive aspects of them working together that you saw, e.g. 'I noticed that you were really good at waiting while Sara coloured the body.'
- Explain that you will photocopy the butterfly for each pair so they have one each in their folder for next week.
- Encourage them to practise working together with other people on things this week and explain that you will ask them about this next week.

Ending (5 minutes)

- Explain that each session will end in the same way each week.
- Ask them to share one thing they have learnt or enjoyed about being in the group today.
- Praise them for their hard work in the session and tell them you will see them at the same time and in the same room next week.
- Walk them back to their class.

Overview: week three

Beginning (10 minutes)

- Encourage each child to colour their chart.
- Check if they remember the ground rules and ask if they want to add to them.
- Ask them to share examples of when they have worked together on things with other people this week and talk about how that felt.

Middle (20 minutes)

- Explain that this week they are going to make something for someone else in the group.
- Ask them to share examples of when they have done this before.
- Put them in pairs and ask them to make a bookmark for the other person.
- Ask them to give the bookmark to the other child and talk about how it feels to make something for someone else and give it to them.
- Encourage each child to thank the other child for making it for them.
- Encourage them to practise being kind to other people this week and explain that you will ask them about this next week.

Ending (5 minutes)

- Explain that each session will end in the same way each week.
- Ask them to share one thing they have learnt or enjoyed about being in the group today.
- Praise them for their hard work in the session and tell them you will see them at the same time and in the same room next week.
- Walk them back to their class.

Facilitator's guide: week three

Beginning (10 minutes)

- Put each child's folder on the table in the same place as last week and put the ground rules up on the wall.
- Encourage them to find their folder and colour in their session chart.
- Acknowledge that you are pleased to see them all again.
- Encourage them to put their session chart in their folder.
- Show them the start and end time on the clock.
- Ask them if they can remember the ground rules and show them.
- Ask if anyone would like to add to the ground rules and remind them that it's ok if they don't want to.
- Ask them to share examples of when they have worked together on things with other people this week and talk about how that felt.

Middle (20 minutes)

- Explain that the task for this week is to make a bookmark for another person in the group.
- Encourage them to think about when they have made something for someone else before and how that felt.
- Introduce concepts of special, cared for, etc. and check they know what they mean.
- Explain that each child will be making a bookmark for someone else and put them in pairs to do this.
- Acknowledge that because everyone in the group is different, they may find that they are not happy with the way someone else has done this, e.g. 'Mark you may look at the picture that Sara has drawn and think you could have drawn it better or not like the way she has drawn it. Being accepting and kind means that even though you may like it to be different you are able to accept it how it is and not make unkind comments about it.'
- Explain that there is no right or wrong way of making the bookmark, but to remember that they are making it for someone else so they can try and think about what the other person may like, e.g. 'If you know that person's favourite colour is red, then we may use that colour as we know they would like it, even though we prefer blue. It is kind to think about other people.'
- Acknowledge that 'This is not an easy thing to do, but in here we are practising new ways of behaving and being able to accept other people being different is one way of us being able to do this.'
- Ask each child to share how it felt making the bookmarks and how they feel about their own bookmarks, reminding them to try and be thoughtful and kind when they are doing this.
- Praise them for being able to do this and acknowledge 'That can be a difficult task to do and you have all managed to be accepting and kind to each other.'
- Ask them to give the bookmark to the person they have made it for and encourage each child to say thank you.
- Encourage them to share how it feels when someone thanks you for something you have done for them.
- Encourage them to put their bookmark in their folder and remind them you will keep their folders until the last week.
- Reflect 'It can be hard when you've made something and want to take it with you today, but I'm going to keep all your things safe for you in your folder.'
- Encourage them to practise being kind to other people this week and explain that you will ask them about this next week.

Ending (5 minutes)

- Explain that each session will end in the same way each week.
- Ask them to share one thing they have learnt or enjoyed about being in the group today.
- Praise them for their hard work in the session and tell them you will see them at the same time and in the same room next week.
- Walk them back to their class.

Overview: week four

Beginning (10 minutes)

- Encourage each child to colour their chart.
- Check if they remember the ground rules and ask if they want to add to them.
- Ask them to share examples of when they have been kind to other people this week and talk about how that felt.

Middle (20 minutes)

- Explain that this week they are going to think of more ways that they can be kind to other people and ask them to share examples with you.
- Ask them to think about different ways we can use our hands in a kind way, e.g. helping someone carry something, opening a door for them, etc.
- Show them the list of words on the table and talk about each one to check their understanding, e.g. caring.
- Give each child a piece of paper and put them into pairs and ask them to draw round each other's hand on the paper, so each child has the other child's hand on their paper.
- Ask them to write 'kind hand' on it and choose a word from the table to glue onto their hand.
- They can colour the hand if there is time.
- Encourage them to practise being helpful to other people this week and explain that you will ask them about this next week.

Ending (5 minutes)

- Explain that each session will end in the same way each week.
- Ask them to share one thing they have learnt or enjoyed about being in the group today.
- Praise them for their hard work in the session and tell them you will see them at the same time and in the same room next week.
- Walk them back to their class.

Facilitator's guide: week four

Beginning (10 minutes)

- Put each child's folder on the table in the same place as last week and put the ground rules up on the wall.
- Encourage them to find their folder and colour in their session chart.
- Acknowledge that you are pleased to see them all again.
- Encourage them to put their session chart in their folder.
- Show them the start and end time on the clock.
- Ask them if they can remember the ground rules and show them.
- Ask if anyone would like to add to the ground rules and remind them that it's ok if they don't want to.

- Ask them to share examples of when they have practised being kind this week and talk about how that felt.

Middle (20 minutes)

- Explain that this week they are going to think of more ways that they can be kind to other people and ask them to share examples with you of ways they can be kind around school, e.g. holding the door open for someone.
- Encourage each child to share an example, reflecting that 'Sometimes it can be hard to think of examples of things we have done.'
- Show them the list of words on the table and talk about each one to check their understanding, e.g. caring.
- Explain that they are going to practise working together again and ask them to remember another time when they have done this in the group.
- Give each child a piece of paper and put them into pairs and ask them to draw round each other's hand on the paper, so each child has the other child's hand on their paper.
- Acknowledge that they will need to help each other with this and practise holding their hand very still while the other person draws round it.
- Reflect that 'It may feel ticklish at first and this is ok.'
- If children are laughing and finding it hard to hold their hand still reflect that 'I can see it's really difficult for you to keep your hand still and not to laugh, its good that you are having fun in here.'
- Ask them to write 'kind hand' on it and help children who may find this difficult by writing or spelling it for them.
- Acknowledge that 'I can help you spell the words and remember it's ok to ask for help if we need it.'
- Encourage each child to choose a word from the table to glue onto their hand that describes the other child whose hand they have drawn round, e.g. 'If you think Oliver is caring then you can choose that word to stick on his hand.'
- Allow them to colour the hand if there is time.
- Encourage them to practise being helpful to other people this week and explain that you will ask them about this next week.

Ending (5 minutes)

- Explain that each session will end in the same way each week.
- Ask them to share one thing they have learnt or enjoyed about being in the group today.
- Praise them for their hard work in the session and tell them you will see them at the same time and in the same room next week.
- Walk them back to their class.

Overview: week five

Beginning (10 minutes)

- Encourage each child to colour their chart.
- Check if they remember the ground rules and ask if they want to add to them.
- Ask them to share examples of when they have been helpful to other people this week and talk about how that felt.

Middle (20 minutes)

- Explain that this week they are going to be looking at pictures of different situations and talking about how they think the people may feel.
- Give each child a scenario sheet and discuss each one with them, encouraging them to talk about what is happening.
- Give each child a set of words and discuss them to make sure each child understands them.
- Ask them to match a word to each picture and glue it in the space underneath.
- Encourage them to draw the facial expression for each one in the face next to it.
- Encourage them to try and notice when other children are being unkind or not being a good friend this week and ask them to practise being a good friend and helping that person. Explain that you will ask them about this next week.

Ending (5 minutes)

- Explain that each session will end in the same way each week.
- Ask them to share one thing they have learnt or enjoyed about being in the group today.
- Praise them for their hard work in the session and tell them you will see them at the same time and in the same room next week.
- Walk them back to their class.

Facilitator's guide: week five

Beginning (10 minutes)

- Put each child's folder on the table in the same place as last week and put the ground rules up on the wall.
- Encourage them to find their folder and colour in their session chart.
- Acknowledge that you are pleased to see them all again.
- Encourage them to put their session chart in their folder.
- Show them the start and end time on the clock.
- Ask them if they can remember the ground rules and show them.
- Ask if anyone would like to add to the ground rules and remind them that it's ok if they don't want to.
- Ask them to share examples of when they have practised being helpful this week and talk about how that felt.

Middle (20 minutes)

- Explain that this week they are going to look at some pictures of different situations and talk about how they think the people may feel.
- Explain that some of the pictures show children being unkind and not being a good friend and encourage them to think about how that may feel.
- Acknowledge that 'It can be hard to think about this and may remind us of times when we have felt left out or upset because someone has been unkind to us.'
- If a child wants to talk about their experience of this, then encourage and support them with this and reflect that 'It can sometimes be hard to talk about times that have been difficult or have made us feel sad, so well done for being brave and doing that.'
- Give each child a scenario sheet and discuss each one with the whole group, encouraging them to talk about what is happening in the pictures.
- If a child is not contributing then reflect that 'Sometimes it can be difficult to see pictures or talk about things that may make us feel sad or upset, but remember in here that it's ok to talk about how we feel if we want to.'
- Give each child a set of words and discuss each one to make sure each child has understood what they mean.
- Explain that some of the words can have similar meanings, e.g. angry or cross, lonely or left out, sad or upset, scared or frightened.
- Give each child a glue stick and encourage them to match one word to each picture and put it in the space underneath the picture.
- If a child looks unsure reflect that 'I can see you looking unsure, maybe you are wondering where to put that word.' Discuss the meaning of the word with them again to check their understanding.
- When they have finished explain that they can draw a face to show the feeling in the box next to each picture.
- Reflect that 'Some of these faces may be hard to draw, but remember in here there is no right or wrong way of doing things.'
- While they are drawing the faces, talk about how they can help the children in the pictures and reflect that 'It can be hard to think of how we can help people sometimes, but I wonder if you can think of what may help to make that person feel better?'
- When they have finished, praise them and acknowledge 'You suggested some really helpful ways to help the children feel better, you are all getting really good at being good friends.'
- Encourage them to try and notice when other children are being unkind or not being a good friend this week and ask them to practise being a good friend by helping that person. Explain that you will ask them about this next week.

Ending (5 minutes)

- Ask them to share one thing they have learnt or enjoyed about being in the group today.
- Praise them for their hard work in the session and tell them you will see them at the same time and in the same room next week.
- Acknowledge that next week will be the last week and reflect 'It may feel a bit sad as we've worked together for a while and I've enjoyed getting to know you all a bit more than I did before we had our group.'
- Walk them back to their class.

Overview: week six

Beginning (10 minutes)

- Encourage each child to colour their chart.
- Check if they remember the ground rules and ask if they want to add to them.
- Ask them to share examples of when they noticed other children were being unkind or not being a good friend this week and ask them to talk about how they were a good friend and helped that person and how that felt.

Middle (20 minutes)

- Ask them if they can remember when they made something for someone else before in the group (bookmarks) and how that felt.
- Give each child a medal cut out of card and explain that they will be making friendship medals for each other this week.
- Ask them to think of why they think the other child is a good friend and to write the reason on the medal. Each medal has '. . . *is a good friend because* . . .' written on it, so the child has to insert the other child's name and put the reason, e.g. 'Jamie is a good friend because he is helpful.'
- Explain that you will write the words for them to copy and ask them to give the medal to the person.
- Encourage each child to put their medal on and show it to the group, reading out what the other child has written on it.
- Ask them to say how they feel.
- Recap on all the friendship qualities you have been working on in the group and encourage them to continue practising all the skills.

Ending (5 minutes)

- Give each child their folder and explain that they can take them with them if they would like to.
- Acknowledge the positive changes that have occurred, e.g. 'I remember when it was hard not to listen when other people were talking, but now you are all really good at it.'
- Acknowledge how hard they have all worked and how much you have enjoyed spending time with them.

Facilitator's guide: week six

Beginning (10 minutes)

- Put each child's folder on the table in the same place as last week and put the ground rules up on the wall.
- Encourage them to find their folder and colour in their session chart.
- Acknowledge that you are pleased to see them all again.
- Encourage them to put their session chart in their folder.

- Show them the start and end time on the clock.
- Ask them if they can remember the ground rules and show them.
- Ask if anyone would like to add to the ground rules and remind them that it's ok if they don't want to.
- Remind them that this is their last week and respond appropriately to any comments they make, e.g. 'I know it may feel sad as we've worked together for six weeks.'
- Recap each week and encourage them to remember the activities. You may want to have a list with you to help you remember.
- While they are doing this you can acknowledge any memorable moments for you, e.g. 'I remember when you did the bookmarks for each other together and you all did so well thinking about how to make them nice for each other.'
- Respond appropriately to any comments the children make about any memories they have by reflecting 'I hear you've got some good memories of our time together in the group too.'

Middle (20 minutes)

- Ask them if they can remember when they made something for someone else before in the group (bookmarks) and how that felt.
- Give each child a medal cut out of card and explain that they will be making a friendship medal for another child in the group this week.
- Reflect 'Remember it can feel really good to do something kind or thoughtful for someone else.'
- Put them in pairs and encourage them to think about the child they have worked with in the group and reflect 'Think about when you may have worked with them on an activity in pairs or with them in the whole group and what you've liked about being in the group with them. Remember it's not a spelling test, I can help you with any words you are unsure about.'
- Encourage each child to put their medal on and show it to the group, reading out what the other child has written on it.
- If a child looks unsure then offer to read it out for them and reflect 'Sometimes we need help from other people and I can help you by reading it out if you would like me to.'
- Ask them to say how they feel.
- Recap on all the friendship qualities you have been working on in the group and encourage them to continue practising all the skills.

Ending (5 minutes)

- Give each child their folder and explain that they can take it with them if they would like to.
- If a child doesn't want to take their folder reflect that 'Maybe you're unsure about taking it back to class with you, you can collect it from the school reception area or office (depending on where is appropriate for your school) at home time if you would prefer to.'
- Acknowledge that 'Sometimes endings can feel sad and I have really enjoyed spending time with you all and you've all worked very hard in here. Although we won't have our group anymore we will still see each other around school, which I know won't be the same, but you can always come and talk to me if you want to.'
- Walk them back to class.

12 Self-esteem programme and facilitator's guidelines

This chapter contains a weekly overview and facilitator's guidelines for each session. The weekly overview provides a summary of each week's session and activities. The facilitator's guidelines are more detailed and provide examples of reflections to use during the sessions. The group facilitator needs to take the facilitator's guidelines with them to each session.

The resources are in the resources section at the end of the book.

Overview: week one

Beginning (10 minutes)

- Introduce the group and explain about the time and number of sessions.
- Encourage each child to sit at the table, put their name sticker on (if applicable), colour their chart and write their name on their folder.
- Explain that you will look after their folder and explain that you will keep everything until the last session when they can take it with them if they want to.
- Explain that the group will start and end in the same way each week, but the activity in the middle will be different.
- Discuss the ground rules for the group, encourage them to contribute their ideas and write them up and display them.

Middle (20 minutes)

- Explain that this week you will be looking at feelings and talking about the different feelings that we all have.
- Explain that you will be reading them a story about different feelings and you will talk about it afterwards.
- Read the story to the group.
- Use the questions for discussion, explaining each one to ensure they have all understood.
- Facilitator to demonstrate facial expressions and encourage children to guess, happy/sad/cross/scared.

Ending (5 minutes)

- Explain that the session will end the same way each week by asking them to share something about themselves. Go round the group and ask each child to say their favourite colour.

Facilitator's guide: week one

Beginning (10 minutes)

- If you already know the children and are not using the name stickers then indicate to the children where you would like them to sit.
- If you are using stickers put each child's name sticker out on the table, ensuring the children who will need the most support are sat next to you.
- Encourage them to find their sticker and sit at the table.
- Reflect that 'It may feel strange coming out of class with me today.'
- Reflect that 'It may feel uncomfortable at first as we don't know each other very well yet, but we will spend the next six weeks getting to know each other better.'
- Discuss that the group is a way of helping them to practise and develop new skills such as sharing, taking turns and being good friends and the activities will provide ways to help them with this.
- Explain that being in this group is a bit different to the rest of school because in here they can choose not to join in the discussions if they do not want to.
- Reflect that 'It's really important that you feel happy being in here and sharing your ideas, some children find this easy and other children find it difficult and that's because we are all different. It's ok in here if you need help with this and you can just say if you do not want to join in our discussions, but this group is to help make this easier for you to do this.'
- If a child is looking round the room then reflect 'I can see you are looking round the room, maybe it feels a bit strange coming in here.'
- Explain that you will see them every week for 6 weeks and if you need to miss a week due to a school trip or you being absent then they will have the session the following week so they will not miss the session.
- Tell them you will see them at the same time on the same day each week and show them on the clock the start and end time.
- Give each child a folder and a session chart.
- Encourage them to colour in week one on their chart and say they can choose which colour to use.
- Ask them to put the chart in their folder when they have finished.
- If a child needs help with this reflect that 'It can be difficult to do this and I wonder if you would like some help with it?'
- Explain that they can write their name however they want to on their folder as it is theirs: 'You can do it in big or small writing wherever you want to as it's your folder.'
- If a child looks unsure reflect that 'It seems like you're not sure where or how to write it, but remember you can choose and there's no right or wrong way.'
- Collect the folders and explain that you will look after them until next week and say 'When you come in next week I will have your folder and colour chart set out waiting for you, just like I did this week. It may feel difficult leaving all your work in here but I will keep it safe for you and you can take everything with you on the last week.'
- Introduce them to the idea of ground rules for the group and encourage each child to contribute if they wish to; allow children to just observe and not contribute if they want to. Reflect that 'It can be hard to think of things to say so don't worry if you can't think of a rule today, we will look at this again next week.'
- Write the ground rules for the group on card and display them so all the children can see them easily.

- Explain that the rules will be up each week to help everyone to follow them.
- Acknowledge that 'It can be hard to remember the rules so this will help us to remember.'

Middle (20 minutes)

- Explain that this week you will be looking at feelings and talking about the different feelings that we all have.
- Acknowledge that we all have feelings and that they can make us feel happy, sad, angry, cross, scared, etc.
- Reflect that 'Sometimes it can feel frightening if we feel angry, cross or upset, but it can help to talk to other people about how we feel, and this is what we are going to practise doing in this group. This might feel a bit hard at first but we will all help each other to do this.'
- Reflect that 'Sometimes it can be really hard to speak, but remember in here you can share your ideas if you want to, and if you don't want to that's ok.'
- Explain that you will be reading them a story about different feelings and you will talk about it afterwards.
- Check they are all comfortable on their seats and help them to move their chairs if they need to.
- Acknowledge that 'It can be hard to sit still and listen to a story if you are not feeling comfortable.'
- Read the story to the group and respond to any emotional responses from the children, e.g. 'I can see you are looking a bit unsure, maybe that story has made you think about lots of different feelings.'
- Read through each question and explain each one to ensure they have all understood them.
- Discuss the children's answers to the questions and ensure you validate each response.
- If a child is not responding or seems unsure, reflect that 'Maybe you're not sure what to say, but in here we can say things even if we are not sure if it is the right answer, because we are just talking about what we thought happened in the story and it doesn't matter if you say something different to the other children. Remember we are all different and we may think and feel different things about the story.'
- Explain that you will use your face to show some different feelings and would like them to try and guess what the feeling might be. Reflect that 'Sometimes it can be difficult to know what people may be feeling from looking at their faces, but you can try and guess and it doesn't matter if you get it wrong. Everyone gets things wrong sometimes and that's ok.'
- Demonstrate each facial expression – happy, sad, cross, scared – and encourage them to guess the feeling after each one.
- If any of the children laugh then acknowledge that 'I'm sure it must look very funny when I am pulling these faces and it's making you laugh.'

Ending (5 minutes)

- Explain that each session will end in the same way each week.
- Ask them to share one thing they have learnt or enjoyed about being in the group today.
- If a child looks uncomfortable or is unsure what to say, reflect that 'It can be hard to think of what to say sometimes, but it can be anything at all that you have liked or enjoyed. Remember it may be different to what someone else has learnt or enjoyed as we will all learn and enjoy different things.'
- Praise them for their hard work in the session and tell them you will see them at the same time and in the same room next week.
- Walk them back to their class.

Overview: week two

Beginning (10 minutes)

- Encourage each child to colour their chart.
- Check if they remember the ground rules and ask if they want to add to them.
- Ask them to recall last week's session and what they did.

Middle (20 minutes)

- Explain that this week you will be talking about things they like.
- Acknowledge that some of the things they like may be the same and some may be different and that's ok because we are all different people.
- Encourage each child to draw a picture of them doing something they like.
- Encourage each child to share their picture with the rest of the group and talk about what they are doing.

Ending (5 minutes)

- Explain that it is the same task as last week, but this week ask each child to say what their favourite food is.

Facilitator's guide: week two

Beginning (10 minutes)

- Put each child's folder on the table in the same place as last week and put the ground rules up on the wall.
- Encourage them to find their folder and colour in their session chart.
- Acknowledge that you are pleased to see them all again.
- Encourage them to put their session chart in their folder.
- Show them the start and end time on the clock.
- Ask them if they can remember the ground rules and show them.
- Ask if anyone would like to add to the ground rules and remind them that it's ok if they don't want to.
- Ask if anyone can remember what they did last week and remind them. Reflect that 'It can be hard to remember what we did last week; a week is a long time.'

Middle (20 minutes)

- Explain that this week you will be talking about things they like and they will be making their own poster.
- Explain that there is no right or wrong way to do this and all the posters will be different. Acknowledge that 'You are all different people and will like different things, some of you may like the same things and some may be different. For example, Jamie may love chocolate and Sara may prefer crisps.'
- Give each child a piece of paper and encourage them to draw something they like.

- If a child appears to be unsure or is looking at another child's picture reflect 'I can see you looking unsure and looking at Paul's picture, maybe you are unsure what to draw, remember it can be anything at all that you like.'
- Encourage each child to hold their picture up and show it to the rest of the group and tell them about their picture and what they like. Reflect that 'Sometimes it can feel uncomfortable showing other people what we have made, but in here we will be doing lots of this and helping each other to get used to doing it.'
- If a child appears anxious or reluctant to do this reflect, 'Sometimes it can feel difficult showing people what we have made, but remember in here we will all be kind to each other and say nice things about each other's work.'
- Encourage the other children in the group to say something they like about the child's picture when they have shown it to them, e.g. 'I like the picture of the swimming pool you've drawn.'

Ending (5 minutes)

- Explain that each session will end in the same way each week.
- Explain that it is the same task as last week, but this week ask each child to say what their favourite food is.
- Praise them for their hard work in the session and tell them you will see them at the same time and in the same room next week.
- Walk them back to their class.

Overview: week three

Beginning (10 minutes)

- Encourage each child to colour their chart.
- Check if they remember the ground rules and ask if they want to add to them.
- Ask them to recall last week's session and what they did.

Middle (20 minutes)

- Explain that this week you will be talking about people being the same and people being different.
- Acknowledge that everyone is different, they may all like different things, and that this is ok.
- Encourage each child to draw pictures of their favourite toy, animal and person on the worksheet.
- Encourage each child to hold their worksheet up for the rest of the group to see and ask them to tell the group about their pictures.

Ending (5 minutes)

- Explain that it is the same task as last week, but this week ask each child to say their favourite drink is.

Facilitator's guide: week three

Beginning (10 minutes)

- Put each child's folder on the table in the same place as last week and put the ground rules up on the wall.
- Encourage them to find their folder and colour in their session chart.
- Acknowledge that you are pleased to see them all again.
- Encourage them to put their session chart in their folder.
- Show them the start and end time on the clock.
- Ask them if they can remember the ground rules and show them.
- Ask if anyone would like to add to the ground rules and remind them that it's ok if they don't want to.
- Ask if anyone can remember what they did last week and remind them. Reflect that 'It can be hard to remember what we did last week; a week is a long time.'

Middle (20 minutes)

- Explain that this week you will be talking about people being the same and people being different.
- Share an example of something that is different between two children in the group, e.g. 'Marcus has blue eyes but Dorcas's eyes are brown.'
- Acknowledge that everyone is different: some people may like the same thing and other people may like different things and that's ok.
- Remind them of the pictures they made last week and acknowledge any differences in the pictures and the things they liked.
- Give each child a worksheet and explain that they can draw their favourite person, toy and animal.
- Explain that they can choose what they would like to draw and that there is no right or wrong way of doing this activity; they can decide what they like best.
- Acknowledge that 'It can feel hard sometimes if we see someone drawing something different to us but remember we may all like different things and that's a good thing.'
- If you see a child looking at another child's worksheet reflect that 'I can see you looking at Luke's cat that he is drawing and maybe you are unsure what to draw. Remember it's important that you think about your favourite things and choose to draw the things that you like best.'
- Ask them to show the worksheet to the other children and tell them about their favourite things.
- If a child looks unsure or anxious you can offer to help them and reflect, 'It can feel difficult talking about ourselves and the things we like sometimes.'

Ending (5 minutes)

- Explain that each session will end in the same way each week.
- Explain that it is the same task as last week, but this week ask each child to say what their favourite drink is.
- Ask them to share one thing they have learnt or enjoyed about being in the group today.
- Praise them for their hard work in the session and tell them you will see them at the same time and in the same room next week.
- Walk them back to their class.

Overview: week four

Beginning (10 minutes)

- Encourage each child to colour their chart.
- Check if they remember the ground rules and ask if they want to add to them.
- Ask them to recall last week's session and what they did.

Middle (20 minutes)

- Explain that this week you will be talking about special qualities that they have.
- Acknowledge that everyone has something that is special about them.
- Give each child a heart and encourage them to decorate it and think of something that is special about them.
- Explain that it can be hard to do this and you will help them with this.
- Encourage each child to show their heart to the rest of the group and ask the group to say something they like about it.

Ending (5 minutes)

- Explain that it is the same task as last week, but this week ask each child to say what their favourite animal is.

Facilitator's guide: week four

Beginning (10 minutes)

- Put each child's folder on the table in the same place as last week and put the ground rules up on the wall.
- Encourage them to find their folder and colour in their session chart.
- Acknowledge that you are pleased to see them all again.
- Encourage them to put their session chart in their folder.
- Show them the start and end time on the clock.
- Ask them if they can remember the ground rules and show them.
- Ask if anyone would like to add to the ground rules and remind them that it's ok if they don't want to.
- Ask if anyone can remember what they did last week and remind them. Reflect 'It can be hard to remember what we did last week; a week is a long time.'

Middle (20 minutes)

- Explain that this week you will be talking about special qualities that they have.
- Acknowledge that everyone has something that is special about them and ask them to think about and share their ideas about what they think this means.
- If they are unsure or you can see a child looking anxious, reflect that 'I can see you are looking a bit unsure so maybe you need some help with that question.'

- Discuss that it may be something that is special about the sort of person they are, such as being kind, thoughtful, helpful, or it may be something that they are good at, such as helping people, being good at reading or playing football.
- Acknowledge that they may all have something different about them that is special and remind them about the activity last week where they looked at things that were different about each other.
- Acknowledge that 'It may be that you are special because you are really good at helping people, but someone else in the group is special because they are really good at swimming. It's good that we are all different because that's what makes us special.'
- Give each child a heart and encourage them to decorate it. While they are doing this tell them that you would like them to think about what they would like to write on it in the space after 'I am special because. . .'
- Acknowledge that it can be hard to do this and reflect, 'Sometimes it can be difficult to think about what makes us special, but I will spend time with each of you and help you to do this.'
- Encourage them to decorate the heart however they like and acknowledge that 'These are for you to decorate and you can do this however you like, there is no right or wrong way of doing this.'
- Spend time with each child encouraging them to think about what is special about them, and to write this on their heart. Offer to help them with spellings and remind them, 'I can help you with spellings, remember I am here to help you.'
- If a child appears to be finding it hard to think about what is special about them give them suggestions such as 'It may be something you enjoy doing or something that other people say you are good at. I wonder what it might be?'
- Encourage each child to suggest their own idea of what they think makes them special, but if they are finding this too hard reflect, 'It seems to be so difficult for you to think of something, I wonder if we could help you to think of something?'
- If you know the child then suggest something you feel is special about them or encourage the other children in the group to help by acknowledging 'I know that you all know Jake and I wondered if we could help him to think of something that is special about him.'
- When all the children have finished their hearts ask them to show them to the rest of the group one at a time.
- Ask the group to say something they like about each heart while they are doing this, e.g. 'I like the colours you have used to decorate it.'

Ending (5 minutes)

- Explain that each session will end in the same way each week.
- Explain that it is the same task as last week, but this week ask each child to say what their favourite animal is.
- Praise them for their hard work in the session and tell them you will see them at the same time and in the same room next week.
- Walk them back to their class.

Overview: week five

Beginning (10 minutes)

- Encourage each child to colour their chart.
- Check if they remember the ground rules and ask if they want to add to them.
- Ask them to recall last week's session and what they did.

Middle (20 minutes)

- Explain that this week you will be talking about feeling proud and making a poster about it.
- Introduce the concept of feeling proud and ask them to think about when they have felt like this.
- Encourage each child to think about and share one thing they are proud of.
- Explain that they are going to be making their own proud poster and give them stars to write on or draw things they are good at and put them on their poster.
- Encourage each child to share their poster with the rest of the group.

Ending (5 minutes)

- Explain that it is the same task as last week, but this week ask each child to say where their favourite place is.

Facilitator's guide: week five

Beginning (10 minutes)

- Put each child's folder on the table in the same place as last week and put the ground rules up on the wall.
- Encourage them to find their folder and colour in their session chart.
- Acknowledge that you are pleased to see them all again.
- Encourage them to put their session chart in their folder.
- Show them the start and end time on the clock.
- Ask them if they can remember the ground rules and show them.
- Ask if anyone would like to add to the ground rules and remind them that it's ok if they don't want to.
- Ask if anyone can remember what they did last week and remind them. Reflect 'It can be hard to remember what we did last week; a week is a long time.'

Middle (20 minutes)

- Explain that this week you will be talking about what makes them feel proud and they will be making their own poster about it.
- Introduce the concept of feeling proud and explore its meaning with the children to ensure they understand, e.g. 'Proud is a word that some of you may know and have heard before.

I wonder if anyone knows what it means? Don't worry if you don't know, we will be talking about it together today to make sure you all understand.'

- If the children are unsure you can offer suggestions to them such as 'Proud means feeling pleased with ourselves when we have done something well or managed to do something that we have found difficult or hard to do.'
- Encourage each child to think about things that they are proud of and reflect that 'It can sometimes feel hard to think about things that we have done well, but we will have some time to think and see if we can think of things and then we will talk about them together.'
- If a child looks anxious or unsure reflect 'I can see you are trying to think of something, it can be anything that you feel you have found hard or difficult but have tried to do, or maybe something that your teacher or another adult has said you have done well or tried hard to do when it hasn't been easy.'
- Ask the children to share one thing they are proud of, ensuring that each child has a turn and supporting children who find it difficult to do by reflecting 'I wonder if you need a bit more time to think, maybe we could go round the group and come back to you if that would help?'
- If a child is still unable to think of anything you can prompt them by reflecting 'I wonder what your teacher or mum or dad would say that you have done well with?'
- Explain that they are each going to make their own proud poster and give them star templates to write or draw on and put on their poster and tell them they will be showing them to the group when they have finished.
- Explain that they can choose whether they write or draw their ideas because this is their poster and they can choose how to make it and what to put on it.
- Remind them you can help them by saying 'Remember I can help you with spellings if you need it.'
- Encourage each child to hold their poster up for the rest of the group to see and reflect that 'It may make you feel proud to be showing your hard work to the rest of the group, there can be lots of things that make us feel proud.'

Ending (5 minutes)

- Explain that each session will end in the same way each week.
- Explain that it is the same task as last week, but this week ask each child to say where their favourite place is.
- Praise them for their hard work in the session and tell them you will see them at the same time and in the same room next week.
- Acknowledge that next week will be the last week and reflect 'It may feel a bit sad as we've worked together for a while and I've enjoyed getting to know you all a bit more than I did before we had our group.'
- Walk them back to their class.

Overview: week six

Beginning (10 minutes)

- Encourage each child to colour their chart.
- Check if they remember the ground rules and ask if they want to add to them.
- Ask them to recall last week's session and what they did.

Middle (20 minutes)

- Explain that this week you will be talking about kind and positive things about each other.
- Set the words out on the table and explain what each one means.
- Give each child a balloon template and ask them to write their name on it.
- Encourage each child to pass round their balloon and ask each child to choose a word from the table to glue on to the child's balloon.
- Ask each child to look at the words on their balloon and say how they feel.
- Encourage each child to decorate their balloon.

Ending (5 minutes)

- Explain that it is the same task as last week, but this week ask each child to say what they would like to be when they grow up.
- Give each child their folder and explain that they can take it with them if they would like to.
- Acknowledge how hard they have all worked and how much you have enjoyed spending time with them.

Facilitator's guide: week six

Beginning (10 minutes)

- Put each child's folder on the table in the same place as last week and put the ground rules up on the wall.
- Encourage them to find their folder and colour in their session chart.
- Acknowledge that you are pleased to see them all again.
- Encourage them to put their session chart in their folder.
- Show them the start and end time on the clock.
- Ask them if they can remember the ground rules and show them.
- Ask if anyone would like to add to the ground rules and remind them that it's ok if they don't want to.
- Ask if anyone can remember what they did last week and remind them. Reflect 'It can be hard to remember what we did last week; a week is a long time.'

Middle (20 minutes)

- Explain that this week you will be talking about kind and positive things about each other and decorating a picture of a balloon with words about each other.
- Set the words out on the table and discuss each one individually to ensure each child understands their meaning, e.g. 'Does anyone know what thoughtful means? What might someone do if they were being thoughtful?'
- Give each child a balloon and ask them to write their name on it. Explain they can write it big or small – it's up to them as it's their balloon.
- Ask them to give it to the child sat next to them.
- Explain that they are going to choose a word from the words that you have talked about on the table to glue on to the child's balloon and ask them to choose a word for that child, e.g. 'If you get Liane's balloon and you think she is helpful then you can choose that word to put on her balloon.'
- If you notice a child is choosing the same word for each, reflect 'I wonder if you can think of a different word to use; let's look at all the words and talk about what they mean again.'
- Pass the balloons round repeating the process of each child choosing a word to glue on each child's balloon until each child gets their own balloon back.
- Ask each child to look at their balloon and read the words out to the rest of the group.
- Encourage them to say how it feels by asking 'I wonder how it feels to hear all those lovely things being said about you by your friends in the group?'
- Encourage them to decorate their balloon.

Ending (5 minutes)

- Explain that each session will end in the same way each week.
- Explain that it is the same task as last week, but this week ask each child to say what they would like to be when they grow up.
- Give each child their folder and explain that they can take them with them if they would like to.
- Acknowledge the positive changes that have occurred, e.g. 'I remember when it was hard not to listen when other people were talking, but now you are all really good at it.'
- Acknowledge how hard they have all worked and how much you have enjoyed spending time with them.
- Give each child their folder and explain that they can take it with them if they would like to.
- If a child doesn't want to take their folder reflect 'Maybe you're unsure about taking it back to class with you, you can collect it from the school reception area or office (depending on where is appropriate for your school) at home time if you would prefer to.'
- Acknowledge that 'Sometimes endings can feel sad and I have really enjoyed spending time with you all and you've all worked very hard in here. Although we won't have our group anymore we will still see each other around school, which I know won't be the same, but you can always come and talk to me if you want to.'
- Walk them back to class.

Conclusion

The impact that good educational practice can have on children and families is invaluable. I hope I have demonstrated that schools have a crucial role to play in developing positive mental health and well-being in children, and in the prevention of further difficulties in adult life and problems for society as a whole. Our prisons and mental health systems have a large percentage of adults who had difficult early experiences as children, which they have carried into their adult lives. We have a responsibility as a society to break the perpetuation of that cycle by providing opportunities for the next generation of young people to have experiences that promote positive mental health and emotional well-being.

There are endless possibilities throughout the school day to introduce emotional vocabulary, provide children with skills and opportunities to express their feelings and produce experiences that enable them to learn about their emotional health and well-being. Schools are in an ideal position to provide children with positive and nurturing relationship experiences, which can provide children with an alternative relational template to the one they may have within their family. When we meet children's emotional and social needs we remove the barriers that create blockages and enable them to learn.

The group work programme is an ideal opportunity to do this in a way that can be easily integrated into the school day with minimal disruption and maximum success. It enables schools to do things differently and provide children with opportunities to experience new ways of understanding and managing their feelings. As adults we may try to protect children from experiencing sadness, hurt and upset, but these are part of life along with happiness, joy and excitement. Our task as practitioners is to support children with understanding and experiencing all feelings, not just some feelings. Children have a strong foundation for later life if they can manage their own feelings, understand the feelings of others and interact positively with other people.

Every child deserves to be happy, safe and settled in school and be equipped with the skills to build friendships, the confidence to do well and the opportunity to reach their full potential. Children need the opportunity to feel they belong, are worthwhile, have something to offer and can make a contribution to the world. Children need to feel they have a purpose in the same way as adults do.

We've got to get it right for children from now. There are generations of children who have had negative experiences of school, resulting in negative views of themselves and taking those experiences into adulthood, therefore increasing the likelihood of ending up in our prisons or mental health systems, having children of their own and repeating the cycle. The long term consequences for individuals, families and society as a whole of children being emotionally unhealthy and having poor relational skills are enormous. We need to take children's mental health seriously. If we invest in children's emotional health and well-being we provide them with potential skills for life; if we don't we provide them with potential problems for life.

Resources

This section contains all the resources needed to prepare, plan and evaluate the group work programs. These can be photocopied and prepared in advance of the programme. The resources include:

- a register
- session notes to be completed at the end of each session
- guidelines for completing intervention questionnaires
- start and end of intervention questionnaires
- a completed example of a group work report
- a blank format of a group work report
- a door sign.

Resources for delivering friendship group:

- overall resources list
- child session chart to be completed each week
- bookmark template
- butterfly template
- kind hands words
- scenarios
- medal template.

Resources for delivering self-esteem:

- overall resources list
- child session chart to be completed each week
- balloon template
- heart template
- kind words for balloon
- star template
- 'My favourite' worksheet
- story and questions.

Group work questionnaires guidelines for group facilitators

- Ask the child's class teacher or teaching assistant to complete the start questionnaires for each child that will be in the group with you.
- Ensure they complete each question and include additional comments about the child and how they are generally in class, at break times and around school. For example, Kevin can be quiet and withdrawn at times or Mia finds it hard to wait her turn and is frequently fighting with other children at lunchtime.
- Ask the same person to complete the end questionnaire for each child, ensuring they complete the section about any other changes that have occurred. For example, Kevin is more confident and is sharing his ideas more in class or Mia is being more patient and is gradually developing more friendships with the other children in the class.
- Compare each question using the start and end questionnaire for each child.
- Identify any positive changes that have occurred in the scoring; for example, a child who could take turns only sometimes but is now able to frequently, along with any comments from the person who completed the end questionnaire.
- List the positive changes and write a paragraph describing how you experienced the child in the group sessions; for example, at first Jamie found it difficult to follow the group rules and kept interrupting while the other children were talking. However, after several gentle reminders and support from the group he was able to do this more easily. He became more confident at sharing his feelings and was able to acknowledge that he felt sad that the group was finishing.

Group work start of intervention questionnaire

Child's name:
Date of birth:

Please complete the following questions based on your knowledge of the child during the last month:

	Yes	No	Sometimes
Is this child able to share?			
Is this child able to make friends easily?			
Is this child kind to other children?			
Is this child able to take turns?			
Does this child have friends?			
Is this child popular?			
Does this child have conflicts with other children?			
Does this child bully other children?			
Does this child do what adults ask?			
Does this child offer to help?			
Does this child tell lies?			
Does this child find it difficult to concentrate?			
Does this child focus and engage with their learning?			
Does this child fidget and appear restless?			
Does this child appear to be anxious, worried or scared?			
Does this child have angry outbursts or tantrums?			
Is this child able to express their feelings easily?			
Does this child appear to be confident?			
Does this child say they feel unwell?			
Does this child appear to be happy?			

Any other comments:

Signed:
Date:

Group work end of intervention questionnaire

Child's name:
Date of birth:

Please complete the following questions based on your knowledge of the child during the last two weeks:

	Yes	No	Sometimes
Is this child able to share?			
Is this child able to make friends easily?			
Is this child kind to other children?			
Is this child able to take turns?			
Does this child have friends?			
Is this child popular?			
Does this child have conflicts with other children?			
Does this child bully other children?			
Does this child do what adults ask?			
Does this child offer to help?			
Does this child tell lies?			
Does this child find it difficult to concentrate?			
Does this child focus and engage with their learning?			
Does this child fidget and appear restless?			
Does this child appear to be anxious, worried or scared?			
Does this child have angry outbursts or tantrums?			
Is this child able to express their feelings easily?			
Does this child appear to be confident?			
Does this child say they feel unwell?			
Does this child appear to be happy?			

Any other changes that have occurred:

Signed:
Date:

Group work report

Child's name: Jodie Bracken	
Date of birth: 25. 6. 09	
Type of group: Friendship	
Group facilitator: Nathan Crompton	
Group dates: January–February 2014	

Questionnaire evaluation:

The questionnaires show that Jodie has made several positive changes since being in the group. She is able to share more easily and is being kinder to other children. Her friendships have improved and she is now more popular. She is no longer telling lies which she was sometimes doing before the group sessions. Her concentration has improved and she is less restless.

Staff comments:

Her class teacher is very pleased with the progress Jodie has made and has noticed that her friendships have improved. She feels she is more confident now and seems to be happier in herself.

Facilitator's comments:

Jodie was a bit quiet and anxious at the start of the group work sessions. She appeared to be worried about making mistakes and would wait for the other children to start before beginning the activity. However, with lots of reassurance she gradually became more confident and started sharing her thoughts and ideas. Her friendships with the other children in the group developed as the sessions progressed.

Recommendations:

Jodie may still need support to help her manage her anxiety about getting things wrong from her class teacher and other adults in school.

Signed:

Date:

Group work report

Child's name:	
Date of birth:	
Type of group:	
Group facilitator:	
Group dates:	
Questionnaire evaluation:	
Staff comments:	
Facilitator's comments:	
Recommendations:	
Signed:	
Date:	

Door sign

Group work in progress

Please do not disturb

Group work register

Please record the date that each group work session takes place and tick whether or not the child attended.

Name of child	Date	Date	Date	Date	Date	Date

Signed ....

Print name ....

Date ....

Group work session notes

Group work facilitator . . . .

Type of group . . . .

Date	Session number	Session detail and comments (it is useful to make notes on individual children and group dynamics)	

Friendship resources

Resources for friendship group

- clock
- register and session record (to be completed each week)
- stickers for children's names if needed (week one)
- folder for each child (all the same colour)
- weekly chart for each child
- felt pens
- lead and coloured pencils
- large card for ground rules
- blu tac for ground rules
- A4 white paper (week one and four)
- butterfly template (week two)
- bookmark template (week three)
- collage materials (week three)
- glue stick (week three and four)
- set of words for each child (week four)
- pictures of scenarios (week five)
- list of words for each child (week five)
- medal template (week six)
- hole punch (week six)
- ribbon for medals (week six).

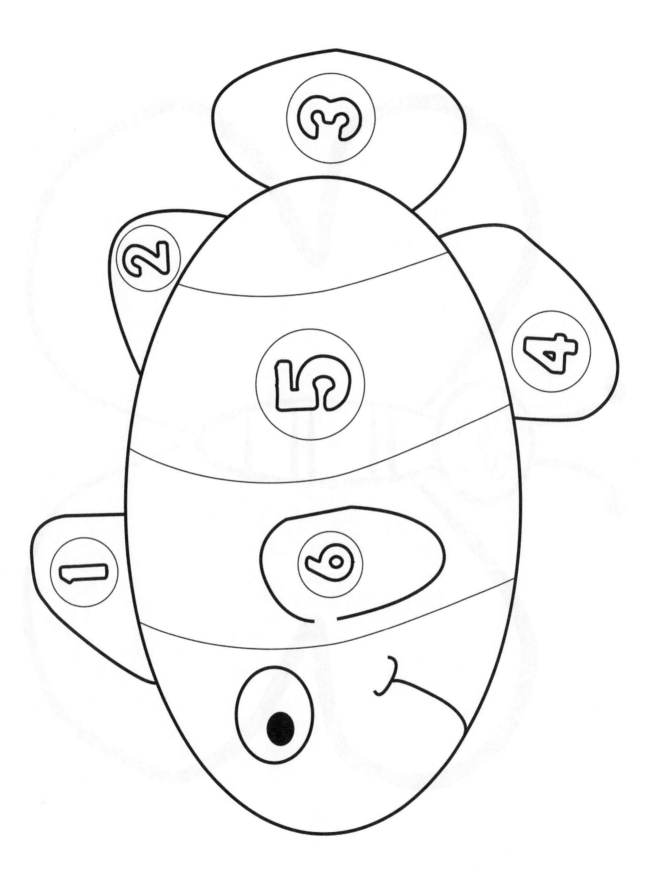

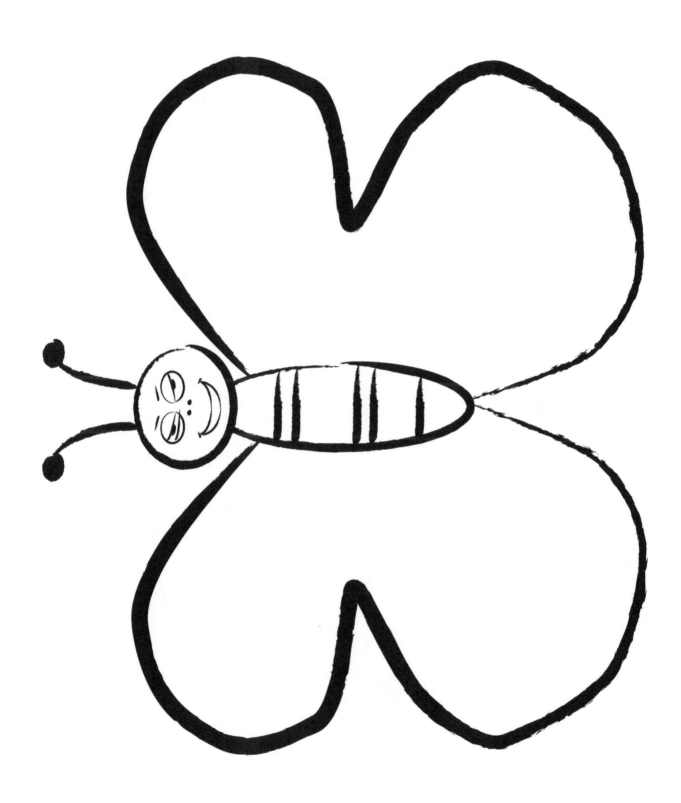

scared

sad

angry

lonely

A child is on their own at play time ◯

A child is crying ◯

A child is hitting another child ◯

A child is shouting at another child ◯

Kind hands

Kind	Kind	Kind	Kind
Helpful	Helpful	Helpful	Helpful
Thoughtful	Thoughtful	Thoughtful	Thoughtful
Caring	Caring	Caring	Caring
Friendly	Friendly	Friendly	Friendly

_____
is a good friend
because....

Self-esteem resources

Resources for self-esteem group

- clock
- register and session record (to be completed each week)
- stickers for children's names if needed (week one)
- folder for each child (all the same colour)
- weekly chart for each child
- felt pens
- lead and coloured pencils
- large card for ground rules
- blu tac for ground rules
- story and questions (week one)
- A4 white paper (week two and week five)
- 'My Favourite' worksheet (week three)
- heart template (week four)
- stars for each child (week five)
- balloon template (week six)
- hole punch (week six)
- ribbon (week six)
- glue sticks (week six)
- list of words for each child (week six).

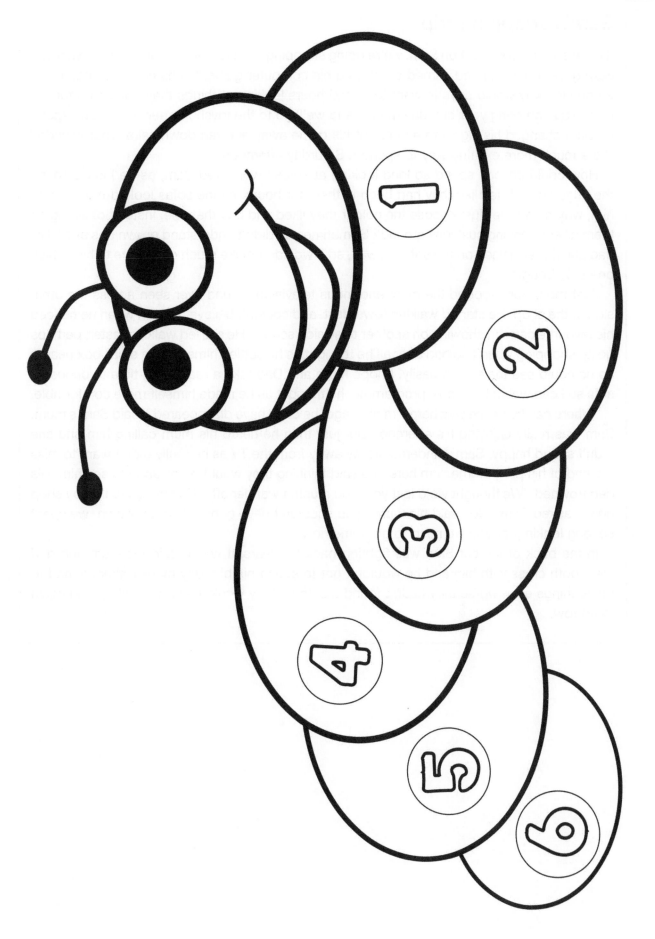

Sam's shopping trip

'Come and get your coat on Sam, we're going shopping,' called Sam's mum from downstairs. Sam gave a big sigh and carried on playing his computer game. He hated shopping; it was so boring, why would anyone want to spend hours looking at things they couldn't afford to buy. 'You can bring your birthday money and we'll go to the toyshop after so you can spend it.' Sam changed his sigh into a grin, put his game away and ran downstairs. That sounded like a much more exciting way to spend a Saturday afternoon.

How could anyone spend so long looking at sofas? wondered Sam, as he looked round the huge shop. It felt like they had been in there for hours. All the sofas looked the same to him, why didn't they just choose the colour they liked and buy that one, instead of sitting on them all and moving cushions around? Sometimes he didn't understand grown ups at all. His dad always fell asleep on the sofa anyway, so it wouldn't make much difference to him which one they bought!

Just then, Sam spotted the most enormous television he had ever seen across the other side of the shop. He started walking towards it, and couldn't believe his luck when he noticed his favourite cartoon showing on another television screen. He started walking faster; perhaps going shopping wasn't so bad after all he thought as he settled himself on a small box nearby so he could see the screen easily. I hope Mum and Dad take a really long time to choose a sofa so I can watch the whole programme, he thought as he made himself more comfortable.

'Where can he be, he was here a minute ago, he can't have disappeared?' said Sam's mum. Sam was really enjoying his afternoon but just then he heard his mum calling him and she didn't sound happy. Sam wandered slowly away from the TV as he really didn't want to miss the end of his programme. 'I'm here,' he said thinking they would be pleased to see him. His dad frowned. 'We thought we'd lost you, you mustn't wander off.' 'Can we go to the toy shop now?' asked Sam. 'No,' said his mum, 'you shouldn't have gone off on your own, we spent so long looking for you we need to go home now.'

In the back of the car Sam was fighting back the tears, it wasn't fair, his mum and dad were both cross with him and he wouldn't get to spend his birthday money after all, and to make things even worse they hadn't found a sofa so they would have to go shopping again tomorrow.

Questions for discussion

- Why didn't Sam like shopping?

- How did Sam's mum and dad feel when they couldn't find him?

- How did Sam feel when they were in the car on the way home?

- Can you think of when you have felt like this?

My Favourite

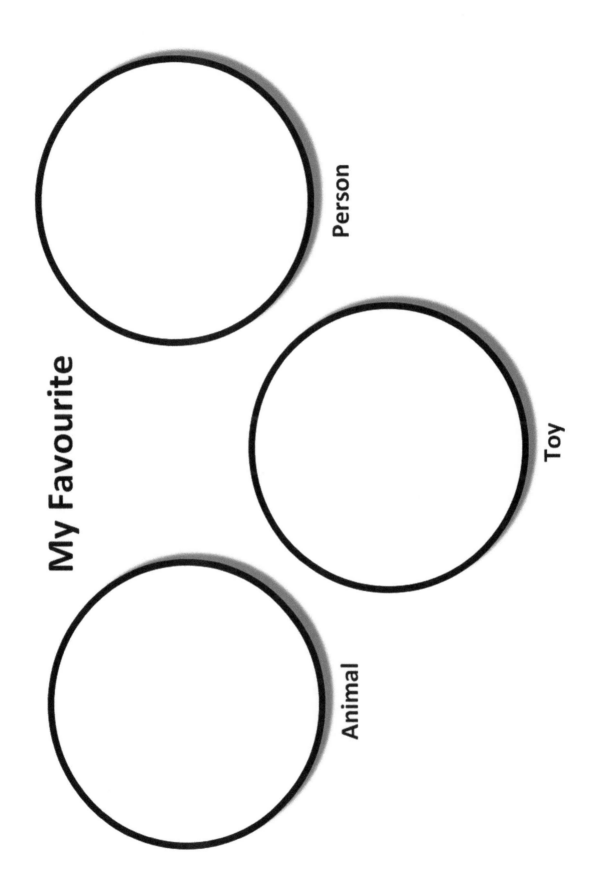

Person

Toy

Animal

I am special because...

Kind words balloon

Thoughtful	Helpful	Kind
Fun	Caring	Friendly
Thoughtful	Helpful	Kind
Fun	Caring	Friendly
Thoughtful	Helpful	Kind
Fun	Caring	Friendly
Thoughtful	Helpful	Kind
Fun	Caring	Friendly

Index